أسماء الله الحسنى

The Excellent Names of God

WITH LEXICAL AND EXEGETICAL NOTES

Translated and Edited By
S.G Mohiduddin

Introduction By
Syed Abul Hasan Ali Nadwi

NADWI PRESS

NADWI PRESS

Nadwi Press Edition

Find our titles on your favourite online bookstore using the keyword 'Nadwi Press'

Originally Published by AIRP, Lucknow (India)
Reprinted by Nadwi Press in 2026

Translation of the Qur'ān

It should be perfectly clear that the Qur'ān is only authentic in its original language, Arabic. Since perfect translation of the Qur'ān is impossible, we have used the translation of the meaning of the Qur'ān throughout the book, as the result is only a crude meaning of the Arabic text.

Qur'ānic verses appear in speech marks proceeded by a reference to the Surah and verse number. Sayings (Hadith) of Prophet Muhammad (saw) appear in inverted commas along with reference to the Hadith Book and its Reporter.

Contents

In the name of Allah, the Compassionate, the Merciful

Introduction

This brochure gives all the Excellent (or beautiful) Names of Allah which either occur in the Qur'an or were taught by the holy Prophet (peace and blessings of God be upon him). God says in the Qur'an:

﴿وَلِلَّهِ ٱلْأَسْمَآءُ ٱلْحُسْنَىٰ فَٱدْعُوهُ بِهَا ۖ﴾

"Allah's are the excellent names, so call Him by them."

[TMQ: Surah Al-A'raf: 180]

All these excellent names add up to 99. In the 28th part of the Qur'an, 14 of these names have been mentioned with such a grandeur of diction that they send anyone reciting the Quranic text into raptures.

﴿سُبْحَٰنَ ٱللَّهِ عَمَّا يُشْرِكُونَ ﴿٢٣﴾ هُوَ ٱللَّهُ ٱلْخَٰلِقُ ٱلْبَارِئُ ٱلْمُصَوِّرُ ۖ لَهُ ٱلْأَسْمَآءُ
ٱلْحُسْنَىٰ ۚ يُسَبِّحُ لَهُۥ مَا فِى ٱلسَّمَٰوَٰتِ وَٱلْأَرْضِ ۖ وَهُوَ ٱلْعَزِيزُ ٱلْحَكِيمُ ﴿٢٤﴾﴾

"Glory be to Allah, above what they associate. He is Allah, the Creator, the Maker, the Fashioner; His are the Names Most Beautiful. Hallows Him whatever is in the heavens and the earth; And He is the Mighty, the Wise."

[TMQ: Surah Al-Hashr: 22-24]

These epithets are not merely for name-sake but convey His excellent attributes and functions (for He is the sole Author of the heavens and the earth and man and also their Preserver), including His Grace and Mercy and Benevolence for His creation. How sweet and admirable is He, and how much worthy of our devotion and allegiance? There is nothing that He does not possess or is not its Master. None can love us more than He, nor can be more just to us. His knowledge encompasses everything, big or small. He is the Originator of all that exists, and there is no difficulty that He cannot solve. Then why should we not love Him, glorify Him, sing His praises, chant His name on every occasion, call Him in every difficulty, pattern our lives as He desires, follow His commands, and cherish Him more than our own lives, parents, and children? Where is then the occasion for offering a prayer or making a supplication or calling upon anyone else save Him?

In order to understand the relationship between God and man it is essential to know about divine attributes since this connexion will depend on the type of His attributes. If we do not know anything about the characteristics and traits of two persons or we are unaware of the cordial or obliging link that binds one with the other, we will never get to the bottom of rapport between the two. The affair between the people, the bond which fastens them to one another, brings the society into existence and is the source of all laws. The nature and characteristics of the individuals lie at the bottom of marked traits of any society or community.

This is the reason why all the religions and the revealed scriptures have given priority as well as emphasis to the divine attributes over the rituals of worship and the code of behaviour governing the relationship between its adherents.

The sublime and magnificent way in which the Qur'an has summed up the attributes and functions of God- His Power and Glory,

Authorship of the world, Beneficence and Mercy, Love and Kindness, Clemency and Forgiveness, Benevolence and Wrath, Transcendence and Nearness and Wisdom and Knowledge-is so vivid in imagery and word painting that it gives a glimpse of the real concept of Divine nature.

﴿وَلِلَّهِ ٱلْمَثَلُ ٱلْأَعْلَىٰ ۚ وَهُوَ ٱلْعَزِيزُ ٱلْحَكِيمُ ۝٦٠﴾

"For Allah is the sublime similitude, and He is the Mighty, the Wise.

[TMQ: Surah An-Nahl: 60]

﴿لَيْسَ كَمِثْلِهِۦ شَىْءٌ ۖ وَهُوَ ٱلسَّمِيعُ ٱلْبَصِيرُ ۝١١﴾

"Nothing whatever is like unto Him, and He is the Hearer, the Beholder."

[TMQ: Surah Ash-Shura: 11]

This is the reason why the Qur'an affirms the divine attributes, functions, and favours one by one, repeatedly and in such detail. Divine attributes are the fountainhead of love and affection. Their assertion and the similitudes and symbols to demonstrate them whet the instincts of attachment and yearning for Him. The divine attributes and the excellent Names mentioned so elaborately in the Qur'an and the hadith have always kindled the fire of love in the hearts of the travellers on the path of spirit, made the gnostics sing His praises, and obliged the believers to bow their heads in submission to Him. Had they not been aware of these, their faith would become a cold formalism instead of an active, living conviction. These attributes enable us to catch a glimpse of reality, make our hearts throb with excitement, bring tears to our eyes, impart a touching fervour to the supplications, and oblige us to set the heart on attaining divine propinquity. Devoid of these emotions, life would become dry and barren; there would be nothing to distinguish between the human and mineral kingdoms.

The history of religion and philosophy tells us that the Greeks believed in God but without any affection for Him[1]. The Greek mythology had been cast in such a mould that it was incapable of producing the feelings of love and attachment, devotion, and dedication for the Divine Being. It was the logical result of their queer doctrine of a nameless God, without qualities, incomprehensible in His essence, and without any power to help or harm anyone. It was only reasonable that a God without any attributes, functions, and power should have become superfluous for human life-it could not give rise to the feelings of love or hope, fear, or turning to Him in the hour of need. Such a concept of God ends in His nullification, making Him an inert Being lacking all authority to intervene in the affairs of the world. The life of a people taking such view of the Divine Being should inevitably be as if there were no God. It is so because in their craze to apply their mind to the process of negations, they overlook the positive process of assertion. All those having an insight into human psychology and philosophy, morals, religion, and spirituality are aware of the fact that a thousand 'nos' cannot be equated with a single 'yes'. In order to generate the sentiments of devotion and dedication, longing and yearning, hope and confidence, supplication and beseechment, one

---

[1] For details see W. E. H. Lecky, History of European Morals, London. 1869, Vol. I, pp. 344-45.

has to know what God is and what His attributes of Sovereignty, Graciousness, and Mercy mean for man.

Thus, we should not be surprised when we are told that the Greeks lacked love and devotion for God; their ritual prayers and religious services were akin to a body without a soul, or that they had no more regard for their God than their elders. A man learns about great inventors and artists of old from the pages of history, but he never has any emotion of adoration and reverence for them. These sentiments are induced when one comes to regard God as the Eternal Lord and Master of this universe and finds himself a tiny speck, utterly feeble and frail before Him.

Greece and a few other Asiatic countries were not content to divest God of His attributes, reducing Him to an abstract concept, but they also took the reverse process of deification of the Divine attributes of benevolence, dispensing mercy, love, nourishment, and providence, and even conjured up the gods of terror, all these as imaginary but perfect beings. The net result was that the Absolute and Almighty God, Creator and Sustainer of the world, was downgraded to an illusive and powerless entity.

Islam avoids both these extremes and describes Him as One deserving all praises, Almighty, capable of conferring any favour or inflicting any harm, the Lord of life and death, health and illness, difficulty and ease, defeat and victory, in short, as the Qur'an says most concisely:

﴿أَلَا لَهُ ٱلْخَلْقُ وَٱلْأَمْرُ ۗ تَبَارَكَ ٱللَّهُ رَبُّ ٱلْعَٰلَمِينَ ﴿٥٤﴾﴾

"Lo! His is the Creation and the command. Blessed is Allah, the Lord of Worlds." [TMQ: Surah Al-A'raf: 54]

Now, we give here the Excellent and Beautiful Names of God which we have come to know from the Qur'an or His Last Messenger Muhammad (on whom be peace and blessings of God), with their English rendering and explanatory notes, since there is a great merit in remembering and reciting these names. This is a treasure not meant for any particular people or race but for the whole of humanity created by Him. Innumerable favours have been conferred by God on each and every individual, and many of them love and adore Him and desire to sing His praises.

Lucknow

S. Abul Hasan Ali Nadwi

1991

Preliminary Remarks

The Excellent Names of Allah, which are His Attributive Names, have been taken from the *Awrad-i-Rahmāni Azkar-i-Subhani* of *Maulānā Ashraf 'Ali Thânwi*. The morals drawn from these Excellent Names have been indicated (against A) by another scholar, *Maulānā Muhammad Qutb-ud-Din,* while explanatory notes (against B) have been provided by Syed Ghulam Mohiuddin.

2. Of the ninety-nine Excellent Names of God, 5 pertain to the category of *Subhan Allah* (Hallowed be Allah), i.e., separative from all imperfections, 68 relate to the praise of God as *Alhamdulillah* (Praise be to Allah), and 21 glorify the Lord as *Allahu Akbar* (Allah is Great).

3. A perusal of the Qur'an reveals the merits of these Exalted Names in the manner detailed below:-

(i) God has Himself glorified and praised Himself in the Qur'an.

(ii) Glorification of God by His Messengers.

(iii) Glorification of God by the angels.

(iv) Glorification of God on the Day of Resurrection and by the dwellers of paradise.

(v) Glorification of God by all creations, like mountains, birds, and all the beings that exist in between the heavens and the earth.

(vi) Approval of those who praise and glorify God.

(vii) Exhortation for praising and glorification of God by all the Beings.

4. The abbreviations used in the notes are as follows:

LL Lane, E. W., Arabic-English Lexicon

AM *Abdul Majid Daryabadi*, "*Tafsir-ul-Qur'an*, Lucknow, 1981-85.

Rgh *Al-Raghib al-Asfahani, Husain b. Muhammad, Al-Mufradat fi Gharib al-Qur'an.*

AYA *'Abdullah Yūsuf 'Ali*, The Meaning of the Glorious Qur'an, Cairo, n. d.

M *Maudūdī, Abul 'Ala*, The Meaning of the Quran. Delhi, 1973-82.

AA *'Abdullah 'Abbās Nadwi*, Vocabulary of the Quran, Jiddah, 1983.

H Hughes, Thomas Patric, A Dictionary of Islam, London, 1885.

A saying of the holy Prophet, recorded in all the six most authentic compilations of hadith, reads:

"ANYONE WHO ENCOMPASSES THESE (EXCELLENT NAMES OF GOD IN HIS MEMORY, FAITH AND PRACTICE) SHALL ENTER PARADISE."

The Exellent Divine Names			
1 هُوَ ٱللَّهُ ٱلَّذِى لَآ إِلَٰهَ إِلَّا هُوَ *Hu-Allāh-ul-lazi lā ilāha illā huwa* He is Allah, there is no God but He.			2 ٱلرَّحْمَٰنُ *Ar-Rahmān-o* The Compassionate
3 ٱلرَّحِيمُ *Ar-Rahim-o* The Merciful	4 ٱلْمَلِكُ *Al-Malik-o* The King	5 ٱلْقُدُّوسُ *Al-Quddūs-o* The Holy	6 ٱلسَّلَٰمُ *As-Salām-o* The Peace
7 ٱلْمُؤْمِنُ *Al-Mūmin-o* The Protector	8 ٱلْمُهَيْمِنُ *Al-Mohaimin-o* The Preserver of Safety	9 ٱلْعَزِيزُ *Al-'Aziz-o* The Mighty	10 ٱلْجَبَّارُ *Al-Jabbār-o* The Irresistible
11 ٱلْمُتَكَبِّرُ *Al-Mutakabbir-o* The Supreme	12 ٱلْخَٰلِقُ *Al-Khāliq-o* The Creator	13 ٱلْبَارِئُ *Al-Bāri-o* The Evolver	14 ٱلْمُصَوِّرُ *Al-Musawwir-o* The Fashioner
15 ٱلْغَفَّارُ *Al-Ghaffār-o* The Most Forgiving	16 ٱلْقَهَّارُ *Al-Qahhār-o* The Subduer	17 ٱلْوَهَّابُ *Al-Wahhāb-o* The Bestower	18 ٱلرَّزَّاقُ *Ar-Razzāq-o* The Provider
19 ٱلْفَتَّاحُ *Al-Fattāh-o* The Great Judge	20 ٱلْعَلِيمُ *Al-'Alim-o* The Knower	21 ٱلْقَابِضُ *Al-Qābiz-o* The Restrainer	22 ٱلْبَاسِطُ *Al-Bāsit-o* The Spreader
23 ٱلْخَافِضُ *Al-Khāfiz-o* The Abaser	24 ٱلرَّافِعُ *Ar-Rāfi-o* The Exalter	25 ٱلْمُعِزُّ *Al-Mu'izz-o* The Honouner	26 ٱلْمُذِلُّ *Al-Muzill-o* The Reducer
27 ٱلسَّمِيعُ *As-Samī'-o* The All-Hearing	28 ٱلْبَصِيرُ *Al-Basīr-o* The All-Seeing	29 ٱلْحَكَمُ *Al-Hakam-o* The Arbitrator	30 ٱلْعَدْلُ *Al-'Adl-o* The Just

31 ٱللَّطِيفُ *Al-Latif-o* The Subtle	32 ٱلْخَبِيرُ *Al-Khabīr-o* The Aware	33 ٱلْحَلِيمُ *Al-Halim-o* The Forbearing	34 ٱلْعَظِيمُ *Al-'Azīm-o* The Supreme
35 ٱلْغَفُورُ *Al-Ghafoor-o* The Most Forgiving	36 ٱلشَّكُورُ *Ash-Shakoor-o* The Appreciative	37 ٱلْعَلِيُّ *Al-'Ali-o* The High	38 ٱلْكَبِيرُ *Al-Kabīr-o* The Great
39 ٱلْحَفِيظُ *Al-Hafiz-o* The Protector	40 ٱلْمُقِيتُ *Al-Muqīt-o* The Controller	41 ٱلْحَسِيبُ *Al-Hasīb-o* The Reckoner	42 ٱلْجَلِيلُ *Al-Jalīl-o* The Majestic
43 ٱلْكَرِيمُ *Al-Karīm-o* The Noble	44 ٱلرَّقِيبُ *Ar-Raqīb-o* The Watcher	45 ٱلْمُجِيبُ *Al-Mujīb-o* The Responsive	46 ٱلْوَاسِعُ *Al-Wāsi'-o* The Bountiful
47 ٱلْحَكِيمُ *Al-Hakīm-o* The Wise	48 ٱلْوَدُودُ *Al-Wadūd-o* The Loving	49 ٱلْمَجِيدُ *Al-Majīd-o* The Glorious	50 ٱلْبَاعِثُ *Al-Bā'is-o* The Sender of Messengers
51 ٱلشَّهِيدُ *As-Shahīd-o* The Witness	52 ٱلْحَقُّ *Al-Haqq-o* The Truth	53 ٱلْوَكِيلُ *Al-Wakīl-o* The Trustee	54 ٱلْقَوِيُّ *Al-Qawī-o* The Mighty
55 ٱلْمَتِينُ *Al-Matīn-o* The Firm	56 ٱلْوَلِيُّ *Al-Wali-o* The Patron	57 ٱلْحَمِيدُ *Al-Hamīd-o* The Praiseworthy	58 ٱلْمُحْصِي *Al-Muhsi-o* The Counter
59 ٱلْمُبْدِئُ *Al-Mubdi-o* The Originator	60 ٱلْمُعِيدُ *Al-Mu'īd-o* The Restorer	61 ٱلْمُحْيِي *Al-Muhyi-o* The Quickener	62 ٱلْمُمِيتُ *Al-Mumīt-o* The Killer

63 اَلْحَيُّ *Al-Haiy-o* The Living	64 اَلْقَيُّومُ *Al-Qayyūm-o* The Sustainer	65 اَلْوَاجِدُ *Al-Wājid-o* The Rich	66 اَلْمَاجِدُ *Al-Mājid-o* The Glorious
67 اَلْوَاحِدُ *Al-Wāhid-o* The One	68 اَلْأَحَدُ *Al-Ahad-o* The One	69 اَلصَّمَدُ *As-Samad-o* The Independent	70 اَلْقَادِرُ *Al-Qādir-o* The Able
71 اَلْمُقْتَدِرُ *Al-Muqtadir-o* The Potent	72 اَلْمُقَدِّمُ *Al-Muqaddim-o* The Advancer	73 اَلْمُؤَخِّرُ *Al-Muakhkhir-o* The Deferrer	74 اَلْأَوَّلُ *Al-Awwal-o* The First
75 اَلْآخِرُ *Al-Akhir-o* The Last	76 اَلظَّاهِرُ *Az-Zāhir-o* The Evident	77 اَلْبَاطِنُ *Al-Bātin-o* The Immanent	78 اَلْوَالِي *Al-Wali-o* The Protector
79 اَلْمُتَعَالِي *Al-Muta'āli-o* The Exalted	80 اَلْبَرُّ *Al-Barr-o* The Benign	81 اَلتَّوَّابُ *At-Tawwāb-o* The Relenting	82 اَلْمُنْتَقِمُ *Al-Muntaqim-o* The Avenger
83 اَلْعَفُوُّ *Al-'Afuw-o* The Pardoning	84 اَلرَّءُوفُ *Ar-Ra'ūf-o* The Tender	85 مَالِكُ الْمُلْكِ ذُو الْجَلَالِ وَالْإِكْرَامِ *Malik-ul-Mulk-i-Zuljalali-wal-Ikrami* Sovereign of Dominion, Owner of Majesty and Beneficence	
86 اَلْمُقْسِطُ *Al-Muqsit-o* The Equitable	87 اَلْجَامِعُ *Al-Jāmi'-o* The Assembler	88 اَلْغَنِيُّ *Al-Ghanī-o* The Self-Sufficing	89 اَلْمُغْنِي *Al-Mughnī-o* The Enricher
90 اَلْمَانِعُ *Al-Māni'-o* The Withholder	91 اَلضَّارُّ *Az-Zarr-o* The Distresser	92 اَلنَّافِعُ *An-Nāfi'-o* The Benefactor	93 اَلنُّورُ *An-Nūr-o* The Light

94 ٱلْحَيُّ *Al-Haiy-o* The Living	95 ٱلْقَيُّومُ *Al-Qayyūm-o* The Sustainer	96 ٱلْوَاجِدُ *Al-Wājid-o* The Rich
98 ٱلْمَاجِدُ *Al-Mājid-o* The Glorious	98 آلرَّشِيدُ *Ar-Rashīd-o* The Right-Minded	99 ٱلصَّبُورُ *As-Sabūr-o* The Patient

The Excellent Names of God

1. He is Allah, there is no God but He. هو الله الذي لا إله إلا هو

Hu-Allah-ul-lai-la ilaha illa huwa

A. Never turn to anyone (for help) except Allah.

B. 'He is Allah' is comparable to 'I am that I am', as God describes himself to Moses in the Torah, i. e., I am beyond all definitions. Allah is a proper noun applied to the Being who 'exists necessarily by Himself, comprising all the attributes of perfection' (and) 'the al being inseparable from it, not derived' (LL). *Al-ilah* is a different word, and there is nothing to show that Allah is a contraction of *Al-ilah*. Actually, it is a noun par excellence. No plural can be formed from it, and it is, according to the best authorities, without derivation. The word connotes all the attributes of perfection and beauty in their infinitude and denotes none but the One and Unique God, the Absolute, Supreme, Perfect, Tender, Mighty, Gracious, Benign, and Compassionate. The English word God, which is the common Teutonic word for a personal object of religious worship.........applied to all superhuman beings of heathen mythologies who exercise power over nature and man and which primarily meant only what is invoked and what is worshipped by sacrifice, can hardly be even an appropriate substitute' (AM).

Allah is known as the *Ismau'z-Zat*, or the 'essential' name of God, while all other titles are considered as *Isma'us-Sifat*, or 'attributes' of the Divine Being.

2. The Compassionate (Ar-Rahman-o) الرحمن

3. The Merciful (Ar-Rahim-o) الرحيم

A. One should be compassionate and merciful to all sentient beings.

B. Both the words *'Rahman* and *Rahim* are derived from *rahman,* signifying 'tenderness requiring the exercise of beneficence' (Rgh) and thus comprising the idea of 'love' and 'mercy'. Both are active participle nouns of different measures denoting the intensiveness of significances. The former denotes tenderness towards all His creatures in general, and the latter towards His worshippers in particular. The Divine attributes of '*Rahmat*' may on analysis be found to have the following as its components- (1) His provision for everything beforehand that could be needed by man in world; (2) His concern for the well-being of man, both in life and death; (3) His tenderness for man's helplessness; and (4) a disposition on His part to deal kindly and generously with man. 'Mercy may imply pity, long-suffering, patience, and forgiveness, all of which the sinner needs and God Most Merciful bestows in abundant measure. But there is a Mercy that goes even before the need arises, the Grace which is ever watchful, and flows from God Most Gracious to all His creatures, protecting them, preserving them, guiding them, and leading them to clearer light and higher life.' (AYA). Thus, the attribute of mercy in *Ar-Rahman* is manifested before man comes into existence in the creation of things that are necessary for his life here, and therefore without his having deserved them, while the same attribute in *Ar-Rahīm* is manifested when man has done something to deserve it.

The importance of these Divine Names can be judged from the fact that they form part of the sentence placed at the beginning of all the chapters of the Quran except one, and which a Muslim is required to recite before doing any work.

4. The King (Al-Malik-o) الملك

A. One should be the master of his own self.

B.

﴿فَتَعَـٰلَى ٱللَّهُ ٱلْمَلِكُ ٱلْحَقُّ﴾

"Exalted is Allah, the True King!" [TMQ Surah Ta-ha: 114]

The sole Authority giving the command and receiving obedience. God is One in the totality of omnipotent and omnipresent action, which acknowledges no rule, standard, or limit, save His own sole and absolute will. It also means that no superiority, no distinction, no preeminence can lawfully be claimed by one creature over the other. He is entitled to give commands and to receive obedience, and which in fact receives obedience; the power which enforces law and justice. (AYA).

5. The Holy (Al-Quddūs-o) القدوس

A. Should abandon everything else than God.

B. The name occurs in the Qur'an.

﴿يُسَبِّحُ لِلَّهِ مَا فِي ٱلسَّمَٰوَٰتِ وَمَا فِي ٱلْأَرْضِ ٱلْمَلِكِ ٱلْقُدُّوسِ ٱلْعَزِيزِ ٱلْحَكِيمِ﴾

"Hallows whatsoever is in the heavens and whatsoever is in the earth, Allah, the Sovereign, the Holy, the Mighty, the Wise" [TMQ Surah Al-Jumu'a: 1]

The Holy is 'above, and opposed to, all evils; replete with positive good' (AM). Human authority may be misused, but in the title 'the Holy One, we postulate a Being free from all stain and evil, and replete with the highest purity (AYA). The concept separates all impurities and imperfections from the Divine Being.

6. The Peace; The Giver of Peace, (As-Salām-o) السلام

A. Should uproot the factors that lead to, and encourage, evil in society, which disturbs peace.

B. God has given this epithet to Himself in verse 59: 23.

'*Salam* has not only the idea of Peace as opposed to conflict, but wholesomeness as opposed to defects' (AYA). The God is thus the source of Peace and Perfection. This attribute of the Divine Being points to the way of adopting goodness at all levels to broaden them as far as possible and to establish good in place of evil in every area of human life, on the individual as well as the social level. In short, this Divine attribute discourages all things that lead to evil ways or obstruct healthy moral life and encourages to spread the peace of mind and happiness in the society as a whole.

7. The Protector; The Guardian of Faith (Al-Mü'min-o) المؤمن

A. One should protect all from danger, vice, perdition, etc., from one's hands and tongue.

B. The Name occurs in verse 59: 23 of the Qur'an, *'Mü'min* is one who entertains faith, who gives faith to others, who is never false to the faith that others place in him' (AYA). If a man voluntarily comes to God, places his faith in Him, and seeks His Guidance to find the Right Path, he is shown the way which gives him peace and happiness. This is because peace and prosperity is conditional in placing one's faith in God and following His Way, for God protects those who intend to walk in the light of the Book of God. They remain safe from wrong notions, wrong thoughts, and wrong acts and their consequences because at every crossroad they come to know the way with the help of that Light. (M)

8. The Preserver of Safety (Al-Muhaimin-o) المهيمن

A. Should keep oneself completely away from sins and immorality.

B. Another title of God occurring in verse 59: 23 of the Qur'an. God is the Preserver of safety, guarding all from danger, corruption, loss, etc. This is an attribute of kindness and benevolence. God's favours are showered on all-

Of the bounties of thy Lord
We bestow freely on all-
These, as well as those:
The bounties of thy Lord
Are not closed (to anyone).

Even the process of destruction in the universe only subserves the demands of providing safety to every creature. The storms in the oceans, the high floods in the rivers, the volcanic eruptions in mountains, the snowfalls over fields, the hot winds of summer, the thunder of the rainy season, and clouds, and hurricanes-all these may not be pleasing. But one should know that but, for all these, the quality of growth and development in the earth would never have displayed itself, on which depends the life of all creatures. All these are the signs of God which should awaken our souls and lead us to a virtuous life, away from all immorality.

9. The Mighty (Al-'Azīz-o) العزيز

A. One ought to exercise control over one's baser self.

B. A title of God aft-repeated in the Qur'an. God is not only good, but He can also carry out His will. Nothing passes in the universe, neither little nor much, nor small nor great, nor good nor evil, nor profitable nor hurtful, nor faith nor infidelity, nor knowledge nor ignorance, nor prosperity nor adversity, nor obedience nor rebellion, but by His determinate decree and will. Man should, therefore, endeavour to exercise control instead of succumbing to his baser self.

10. The Irresistible; The Mender (Al-Jabbar-o) الجبار

A. One should avoid to become autocratic, which is not befitting for a creature and indeed proves harmful to him.

B. The title occurs only in verse 59:23. One whose will cannot be resisted. Derived from *jabr* which also means the mender of the universe through His will which cannot be resisted, *Jabbar* is 'one who sets bones, or reduces them from a fractured state, a bone-setter: *Jabbar* as applied to God, may mean the Restorer of the poor to wealth or competence or sufficiency (LL).' It also carries the sense of might.

11. The Supreme, The Majestic (Al-Mutakabbir-o) المتكبر

A. One should attach little importance to the world and all that it contains.

B. The epithet occurring in verse 59: 23 of the Qur'an means that God is Supreme above all things and creatures. It is an attribute not shared by any creature, for everything is helpless before God. A life of ease and plenty is nothing to boast of. There were many such in the past which are mere names now. By the same token, the conveniences and good things of life, granted by God, have their uses but they are fleeting and their value is infinitely lower than that of truth and justice and spiritual well-being, the gifts which come from the One who is truly Supreme and Majestic. No wise soul will therefore ascribe greatness to it which belongs only to the Supreme being.

12. The Creator (Al-Khaliq-o) الخالق

13. The Evolver (Al-Bari-o) الباري

14. The Fashioner (Al-Musawwir-o) المصور

A. One should endeavour to attain the perfection of his inner self and the knowledge of Truth.

B. All things in the heavens and on the earth are created by the will of God through a process which does not merely create and leave them alone. He goes on fashioning, evolving new forms, making them perfect and sustaining all the energies and capacities which He has put into His creation, according to various laws established by Him. The act of creation indicated by the three attributive names of God mentioned in verse 59: 24 summarises this process. *Khaliq* is the Author of all creation. He is the final basis of creation; the Cause of all causes; without any pre-existing matter or circumstances. *Bara'a* implies a process of designing and evolving from the previously created matter or state; the Author of this process is *Bārī-o*, the Evolver according to his pre-determined design or plan. *Sawwara* implies giving definite form, shape or colour; so as to make it exactly suited to a given end or object hence the title *Musawwir*, Bestower of forms or colours for this shows the completion of the visible stage of creation. (AYA-M)

15. The Most Forgiving (Al-Ghaffar-o) الغفار

A. One should be ever willing to forgive others.

B. An oft-repeated title of God in the Qur'an. Ghaffar is the emphatic intensive form signifying One who, as depicted by the Qur'an, is vast and unlimited. However serious the sin committed, whatever the nature of one's wickedness and whatever the period in which one has lived in sin, the moment one feels repentant and sincerely knocks at the door of mercy, the response is forgiveness.

﴿۞قُلْ يَٰعِبَادِيَ ٱلَّذِينَ أَسْرَفُواْ عَلَىٰٓ أَنفُسِهِمْ لَا تَقْنَطُواْ مِن رَّحْمَةِ ٱللَّهِۚ إِنَّ ٱللَّهَ يَغْفِرُ ٱلذُّنُوبَ جَمِيعًاۚ إِنَّهُۥ هُوَ ٱلْغَفُورُ ٱلرَّحِيمُ ٥٣﴾

"O My servants, who have transgressed to your own hurt, despair not of God's Mercy, for all sins doth God forgive. Gracious, Merciful is He" [TMQ Surah Az-Zumar: 53]

"This is the perennial theme of the Qur'an. Of course, the Qur'an does not call on man to love his enemy; but it calls on him to exercise forgiveness, for, he who learns to forgive his enemies deserves forgiveness from God."

﴿وَإِن تَعْفُواْ وَتَصْفَحُواْ وَتَغْفِرُواْ فَإِنَّ ٱللَّهَ غَفُورٌ رَّحِيمٌ ١٤﴾

"And, if you pardon and pass over and forgive, then surely Allah is Forgiving, Merciful." [TMQ Surah At-Tagabun: 14]

16. The Subduer, The Dominant (Al-Qahhar-o) القهار

A. One should subdue his baser self and the promptings of Satan.

B. 'The Subduer of His creatures by His sovereign authority and power, and the disposer of them as He pleaseth, with and against their will' (LL). The epithet applied to God denotes that He possesses real and irresistible power, whose mercy and loving-kindness are not to be bought at the expense of His supreme majesty. An epithet signifying Majesty of God which occurs in a few verses of the Qur'an e.g.,

﴿ءَأَرْبَابٌ مُّتَفَرِّقُونَ خَيْرٌ أَمِ ٱللَّهُ ٱلْوَٰحِدُ ٱلْقَهَّارُ﴿٣٩﴾﴾

"Are sundry lords better or Allah the One, the Subduer"

[TMQ Surah Yusuf: 39]

17. The Bestower (Al-Wahhab-o) الوهاب

A. One should be willing to sacrifice one's life and all that he possesses in the way of God.

B. A title occurring in the Qur'an, e.g.

﴿إِنَّكَ أَنتَ ٱلْوَهَّابُ﴿٨﴾﴾

"Surely it is Thou who art the Bestower." [TMQ Surah Al-Imran: 8]

An intensive noun from *Wahaba* meaning to grant, to give as a gift, to dedicate, to offer as a present or to bestow, the title applied to God signifies that He bestows all gifts and favours out of His mercy since whatever good comes to man from God it comes as a mere favour, and not as a matter of right on the part of anyone.

18. The Provider (Ar-Razzaq-o) الرزاق

A. One should provide sustenance to his dependents and impart knowledge to the seekers.

B. The Provider of livelihood, since all the fine and varied things provided for man and other living creatures on land and in sea and air, in the vegetable, animal, and mineral kingdoms have been provided by God alone. 'His bounty is inexhaustible, and He gives to all; but He does not give to all in the same measure because, out of

His fullness of knowledge and wisdom, He can judge best what is best for any of His creatures' (AYA). This epithet has very often been referred to in the Qur'an as for example, in verse 17:30, which says,

﴿إِنَّ رَبَّكَ يَبْسُطُ ٱلرِّزْقَ لِمَن يَشَآءُ وَيَقْدِرُ﴾

"Verily thy Lord extends the provision for whom He will and measures it out," [TMQ Surah Israel: 30]

i.e., give it adapted to one's circumstances in accordance with His pleasure.

19. The Great Judge (Al-Fattah-o) الفتاح

A. Allow others to be benefited by one's knowledge and wisdom and decide disputes with justice.

B. The title has been used only once in the Qur'an.

﴿وَهُوَ ٱلْفَتَّاحُ ٱلْعَلِيمُ ٢٦﴾

"And He is the Great Judge, the Knower." [TMQ Surah Saba: 26]

Derived from the root *fataha,* meaning to open, to disclose, to judge or to decide (besides to grant victory or to conquer), this title of God signifies 'The Judge; or, the Opener of the gates of sustenance and of mercy to His servants' (LL).

20. The Knower (Al-'Alim-o) العليم

A. One should acquire knowledge that is useful.

B. An epithet of God is often repeated in the Qur'an to signify that He is the possessor of infinite knowledge. He knows 'whatever comes to pass, from the extremities of the earth to the highest heavens. Even the weight of a pismire could not escape Him either in earth or heaven; but He would perceive the creeping of the black pismire in the dark night upon the hard stone, and discern the motion of an atom in the open air. He knows what is secret and one conceals it, and views the conception of the minds, and the motions of the thoughts, and the inmost recesses of secrets, by a knowledge ancient and eternal (H)'.

21. The Restrainer (Al-Qabiz-o) القابض

A. One should restrain his vain desires.

8. A derivative form of *qabaza*, which means to seize, to grasp, to contract or retrain. The epithet *Al-Qābiz-o* for God signifies that He is fully competent to tighten the means of subsistence as, for example,

﴿وَٱللَّهُ يَقۡبِضُ وَيَبۡصُۜطُ وَإِلَيۡهِ تُرۡجَعُونَ ٢٤٥﴾

"and Allah scanteth and amplifieth" [TMQ Surah Al-Baqara: 245]

22. The Spreader (Al-Basit-o) الباسط

A. Should fulfil one's legitimate desires.

B. Derived from *basata,* meaning to spread, to widen, etc., the title Al-Basit-o applied to God means One who spreads or widens as

﴿إِنَّ رَبَّكَ يَبْسُطُ ٱلرِّزْقَ لِمَن يَشَآءُ﴾

"Verily, thy Lord extends the provision for whom He will."

[TMQ Surah Israel: 30]

The moral drawn is that one need not unnecessarily curtail his legitimate desire or practice asceticism.

23. The Abaser (Al-Khafiz-o) الخافض

A. One should cast down that which is unjust.

B. The epithet as such has not been mentioned in the Qur'an, but the idea occurs in verses 56:1-3, which says that:

﴿إِذَا وَقَعَتِ ٱلْوَاقِعَةُ ۝١ لَيْسَ لِوَقْعَتِهَا كَاذِبَةٌ ۝٢ خَافِضَةٌ رَّافِعَةٌ ۝٣﴾

"When the Day of Judgement comes some will be abased and others exalted."

[TMQ Surah Al-Waqia: 1-3]

24. The Exalter (Ar-Raf'e-o) الرافع

A. One should exalt or raise that which is just and right.

B. This title too does not find a place in the Qur'an but the idea occurs at several places viz.,

﴿وَهُوَ ٱلَّذِى جَعَلَكُمْ خَلَٰٓئِفَ ٱلْأَرْضِ وَرَفَعَ بَعْضَكُمْ فَوْقَ بَعْضٍ دَرَجَٰتٍ﴾

"And He it is Who has made you vicegerents on the earth, and has raised some of you over others in degrees" [TMQ Surah Al-An'am: 165]

and

﴿وَرَفَعْنَا بَعْضَهُمْ فَوْقَ بَعْضٍ دَرَجَٰتٍ﴾

"We have raised some of them over the others in degrees"

[TMQ Surah Az-Zukhruf: 32]

25. The Honourer (Al-Mu'izz-o) المعز

A. Should acclaim the righteous.

B. Everything is in the hands of God, who with His infinite knowledge and wisdom bestows honour or withdraws it. The Qur'an says,

﴿وَتُعِزُّ مَن تَشَآءُ وَتُذِلُّ مَن تَشَآءُ﴾

"Thou exaltest whom Thou wilt and Thou abasest whom Thou wilt."

[TMQ Surah Al-Imran: 26]

26. The Reducer (Al-Muzill-o) المذل

A. One ought to humiliate the wrongdoers.

B. This epithet does not occur in the Qur'an, but the verb is frequently used, viz.,

﴿وَضُرِبَتْ عَلَيْهِمُ ٱلذِّلَّةُ وَٱلْمَسْكَنَةُ﴾

"And humiliation and wretchedness were stamped upon them."

[TMQ Surah Al-Baqara: 61]

The name is derived from the root *zalla,* meaning to be low, contemptible, submissive, and humiliated. Humiliation is the natural outcome of wrongdoing, and hence, such persons ought not to be paid respect because of their riches or office.

27. The All-Hearing (As-Sam'i-o) السميع

28. The All-Seeing (Al-Basir-o) البصير

A. One should see and hear only that which is good and permissible.

B. 'No audible object, how still soever, escapes His hearing; nor is anything visible so small as to escape His sight; for distance is no hindrance to His hearing, nor darkness to His sight. He sees without eyes and hears without ears for His attributes are not like those of His creatures, any more than His essence is like theirs' (H).

The two titles, oft-repeated in the Qur'an, indicate God's omnipresence.

29. The Arbitrator (Al-Hakam-o) الحكم

30. The Just (Al-'Adl-o) العدل

A. Should judge equitably in all matters.

B. These epithets do not occur in the Qur'an, but they find a place in the attributive titles of the Divine Being mentioned in the Traditions. However, God's justice has been referred to in the Qur'an at several places as, e.g.,

﴿مَٰلِكِ يَوۡمِ ٱلدِّينِ ٤﴾

"*Master of the Day of Judgement*" [TMQ Surah Al-Fatiha: 4]

﴿إِنَّ ٱللَّهَ لَا يَظۡلِمُ مِثۡقَالَ ذَرَّةٖۖ﴾

"God is never unjust in the least degree" [TMQ Surah An-Nisaa: 40]

﴿وَنَضَعُ ٱلۡمَوَٰزِينَ ٱلۡقِسۡطَ لِيَوۡمِ ٱلۡقِيَٰمَةِ فَلَا تُظۡلَمُ نَفۡسٞ شَيۡـٔٗاۖ﴾

"We shall set up scales of justice for the Day of Judgement, so that not a soul will be dealt with unjustly in the least" [TMQ Surah Al-Anbiyaa: 47]

﴿أَلَيۡسَ ٱللَّهُ بِأَحۡكَمِ ٱلۡحَٰكِمِينَ ٨﴾

"Is God not the Wisest of the judges?" [TMQ Surah At-Tin: 8]

etc.

Justice, or *Adl* in Arabic, means to make even or in the sense whereby the two sides of a scale are made to show equal weight. Thus, justice, according to the Quranic concept, introduces balance in the universe, and that it contains and produces unity and harmony. And the sky:

﴿وَٱلسَّمَآءَ رَفَعَهَا وَوَضَعَ ٱلۡمِيزَانَ ٧ أَلَّا تَطۡغَوۡاْ فِي ٱلۡمِيزَانِ ٨﴾

"He has elevated it and set the balance, that you should not trespass in respect of the balance." [TMQ Surah Ar-Rahman: 7-8]

It is this principle or Divine attribute which is responsible for beauty and proportion in every form of life.

The Qur'an speaks of the Divine justice in conjunction with the attribute of Divine mercy it does not isolate justice from mercy, but regards justice as mercy itself. It also says that Divine justice is not something arbitrarily imposed; everyone must win his own redemption. There is no room for any 'original sin', nor for 'universal redemption'. Says the Qur'an:

﴿مَّنْ عَمِلَ صَٰلِحًا فَلِنَفْسِهِۦ ۖ وَمَنْ أَسَآءَ فَعَلَيْهَا ۗ وَمَا رَبُّكَ بِظَلَّٰمٍ لِّلْعَبِيدِ ﴿٤٦﴾﴾

"Whoever works righteously it is for his own soul, and whoever works evil it is against his own soul. Nor is thy Lord ever unjust (in the least) to His servants" [TMQ Surah Fussilat: 46]

31. The Subtle (Al-Latif-o) اللطيف

A. One should be lenient.

B. God is invisible to the eyes and imperceptible to the senses, but He is aware of the subtleties and niceties of all things and affairs in accordance with His perfect wisdom. *Latif* is also 'gentle and benignant,' and when used with the article Al for God, it means the Kind One. The title also means the Gentle e.g.,

﴿ٱللَّهُ لَطِيفٌۢ بِعِبَادِهِۦ﴾

"Allah is Gentle to His bondsmen." [TMQ Surah Ash-Shura: 19]

32. The Aware (Al-Khabir-o) الخبير

A. Should be aware of happenings.

B. A title occurring in the Qur'an e.g.,

﴿وَهُوَ ٱللَّطِيفُ ٱلْخَبِيرُ ﴿١٤﴾﴾

"He is the Subtle, the Aware." [TMQ Surah Al-Mulk: 14]

God is aware of all things and events, whether hidden or manifest. Events past and future are known to Him. He becomes aware of what enters the heart of a man and what he utters with his mouth or conceals. He is free from forgetfulness, negligence or error. His knowledge is eternal; it is not posterior to His essence.

33. The Forbearing, The Clement (Al-Halim-o) الحليم

A. One should be mild and gentle.

B. The word *hilm* means to be mild, clement, and forbearing, restraining oneself at a time when the spirit is roused to anger. The Qur'an repeatedly refers to this attribute of God, signifying that God does not punish the wrongdoers immediately and even defers it to the Day of Judgement fest the sinner might repent and He may forgive him. Attributes like forbearance, benevolence, and forgiveness are concomitants of Divine mercy. The epithet appears at numerous places in the Quran, as e.g.,

﴿وَٱللَّهُ شَكُورٌ حَلِيمٌ ١٧﴾

"And Allah is Appreciative, Forbearing. [TMQ Surah At-Tagabun: 17]

34. The Supreme, The Mighty (Al-Azim-o) العظيم

A. Should be assiduous in acquiring knowledge of the Divine Commands.

B. *Azim* means the mighty, the great; when employed with *Al*, it signifies the Supreme Being, i. e., above all imperfections and immeasurably and eternally exalted and dissimilar to anything conceivable. To Him belongs the power and the might, and His is the dominion and excellency, and the creation and the command thereof.

﴿وَهُوَ ٱلْعَلِيُّ ٱلْعَظِيمُ ﴿٢٥٥﴾﴾

"He is the High, the Supreme" [TMQ Surah Al-Baqara: 255]

﴿رَبُّ ٱلْعَرْشِ ٱلْعَظِيمِ ﴿١٢٩﴾﴾

"Lord of the mighty Throne" [TMQ Surah At-Tauba: 129]

and

﴿ذُو ٱلْفَضْلِ ٱلْعَظِيمِ ﴿١٠٥﴾﴾

"Possessor of the mighty grace" [TMQ Surah Al-Baqara: 105]

35. The Most Forgiving (Al-Ghafoor-o) الغفور

A. One should pardon others for their mistakes.

B. *Al-Ghafoor* has exactly the same meaning as *Al-Ghaffar*. The two epithets for the same attribute, oft-repeated in the Qur'an, indicate the emphasis God wants to place on this quality to be imbibed by the believers, and of which an example unparalleled in the history of the world has been set by the holy Prophet. The people who had not only been guilty of the gravest atrocities against his own person but had also wrought many other wicked deeds and deserved to be severely punished, were forgiven on the occasion of the conquest of Mecca by the holy Prophet with a magnanimity unknown to man. It was done to the tyrants who were at the mercy of the Prophet, at the time of greatest excitement and when his own companions would have rightfully expected him not only to take lawful revenge but also to restore their lost property to them. And this was not all. Before his departure from this fleeting world, the Prophet was asked, through a revelation at the very place he had had to face all those atrocities, to pray for the forgiveness (verse 110:3) of all despite the enormities and sins which the Meccans had committed before accepting Islam against the Divine Being. This incident amply elucidates the Quranic concept of forgiveness:

﴿كَتَبَ رَبُّكُمْ عَلَىٰ نَفْسِهِ ٱلرَّحْمَةَ أَنَّهُۥ مَنْ عَمِلَ مِنكُمْ سُوٓءًۢا بِجَهَـٰلَةٍ ثُمَّ تَابَ مِنۢ بَعْدِهِۦ وَأَصْلَحَ فَأَنَّهُۥ غَفُورٌ رَّحِيمٌ ﴿٥٤﴾﴾

"Your Lord has prescribed mercy on Himself; so that any of you who does an evil through ignorance and then repents and amends, then verily He is Forgiving, Merciful." [TMQ Surah Al-An'am: 54]

36. The Appreciative (As-Shakoor-o) الشكور

A. Should be thankful to God for His grace.

B. Derived from the root *shakara* which means: (1) to give thanks, become grateful, and (2) to be appreciative, being bountiful in giving a reward, this intensive epithet as applied to God signifies, 'He who gives large rewards for small, or few, works' (LL) or, 'one who highly appreciates good and is bountiful in rewarding it.' (AA). The Quran says:

﴿وَمَن تَطَوَّعَ خَيْرًا فَإِنَّ ٱللَّهَ شَاكِرٌ عَلِيمٌ ﴿١٥٨﴾﴾

"And whoso does good voluntarily, then surely Allah is Appreciative, Knowing" [TMQ Surah Al-Baqara: 158]

i. e., surely Allah is ever bountiful in rewarding all good deeds performed with the sincerity of purpose, for He is aware of the innermost thoughts of the doer.

37. The High (Al-'Ali-o) العلي

38. The Great; The Exalted (Al Kabīr-o) الكبير

A. Do not feel humble and lowly in the presence of others.

B.

﴿وَأَنَّ ٱللَّهَ هُوَ ٱلْعَلِيُّ ٱلْكَبِيرُ ۝٦٢﴾

"Verily Allah; He is the High, the Great" [TMQ Surah Al-Hajj: 62]

The God of Islam is the Universal Patron, the All-in-All, Ruler and Protector. He can do anything and is not bound by any conditions or by any coequal entities. This refutes in toto the position of deists and others who have restricted the Divine activity to the creation of the world and fixation of its primary collocations, and also the doctrine of those like Arya Samaj, who conceive God as no other than 'a great cosmic Executive, whose business it is to preside over the inexorable process of transmigration and karma. In Greece, the power even of the highest god was limited, and overruling fate then became an inexorable law, before which even he must bow. Not a tribal deity, nor the national God, nor yet 'Lord of the Hosts', or the anthropomorphic 'our Father in Heaven', the God of Islam rules and sways the world' (AM). He is Living, Powerful, Mighty, Omnipotent, not liable to any defect or limitation, and eternally Exalted. The Supreme Being is the only Agent, the only Force, the only Act existing throughout the universe; the rest is downright instrumentality, from the highest archangel down to the simplest atom of creation.

39. The Protector, The Guardian (Al-Hafiz-o) الحفيظ

A. Guard the limits set by the *Shari'ah.*

B. The epithet does not occur in the Qur'an, but it reminds man, at several places, that God alone protects and guards all creations, for without a constant care and guarding eye, the marvellous order, beauty, and harmony, on a scale of grandeur which we appreciate more and more as our knowledge increases, would not last even for a day. 'Taking the physical heavens, we can imagine the supreme melody or harmony, the Music of the Spheres-- guarded from every disturbing force.' (AYA)

﴿وَلَقَدْ جَعَلْنَا فِي ٱلسَّمَآءِ بُرُوجًا وَزَيَّنَّٰهَا لِلنَّٰظِرِينَ ١٦ وَحَفِظْنَٰهَا مِن كُلِّ شَيْطَٰنٍ رَّجِيمٍ ١٧﴾

"And assuredly We have set constellations in the heaven and made it fairseeming to the onlookers. And We have guarded it from every Satan accursed." [TMQ Surah Al-Hijr: 16-17]

And again;

﴿وَرَبُّكَ عَلَىٰ كُلِّ شَيْءٍ حَفِيظٌ ﴿٢١﴾﴾

"And thy Lord doth watch over all things" [TMQ Surah Al-Saba: 21]

says the Qur'an to describe the guardianship of Allah for His creation.

40. The Controller, The Provider. (Al-Muqit-o) المقيت

A. Should feed the hungry.

B. An epithet of the Divine Being referred to in verse 8:88 of the Qur'an:

﴿وَهُوَ عَلَىٰ كُلِّ شَيْءٍ قَدِيرٌ﴾

"And verily Allah is Controller of everything." [TMQ Surah Al-Mulk: 1]

The word *Muqit,* lit. means capable, overseer and controller, as well as provider and sustainer. The verse cited here carries all the different shades of meanings inherent in *Al-Muqit* since God has power over all things.

41. The Reckoner (Al-Hasīb-o) الحسيب

A. Should help others in their needs and continue to introspect over one's deeds.

B. The title does not occur in the Qur'an, which, however, refers to Him as the Reckoner of all deeds, viz.,

﴿وَكَفَىٰ بِٱللَّهِ حَسِيبًا ﴿٣٩﴾﴾

"And Allah suffices as a Reckoner. [TMQ Surah Al-Ahzab: 39]

God is not only the Master of the Day of Judgement when all men shall be finally requited according to their actions, but God also keeps a watch over all and has full authority to punish them even in this world. It is only the righteousness in the eyes of God (who also knows the intention with which anything is done) that matters, and hence it is necessary that one should always keep on examining one's own deeds, thoughts, and feelings.

42. The Majestic (Al-Jalil-o) الجليل

A. Should attain self-perfection.

B. God is Majestic since He is perfect and compels every being to pay honour to Him. Everything else, even those most magnificent, are but fleeting. 'Empires, the wonders of Science and Arts, the splendours of human glory or intellect will pass away. The most magnificent objects in outer Nature- the mountains and valleys, the sun and moon, the constellation Orion, and the star Sirius-will pass away in their appointed time (AYA) as nothing is perfect. Only God's glory, His Being, Essence, and Attributes are perfect and majestic, which will last forever and compel every creation to pay honour to Him.

43. The Noble, The Bountiful (Al-Karim-o) الكريم

A. One should be gracious and magnanimous.

B. The epithet signifies generosity, kindness, beneficence, graciousness, and concord and has been used in the Qur'an, as an adjective to God as well as the Prophet, Gabriel, the Qur'an, the

Throne of Majesty, etc. According to the contents and its place in a phrase, the different shades of the meaning of the word would be chosen to suit the context (AA). A few examples are:

﴿مَلَكٌ كَرِيمٌ ٣١﴾

"A noble angel" [TMQ Surah Yusuf: 31]

﴿رَسُولٌ كَرِيمٌ ١٧﴾

"A noble Messenger" [TMQ Surah Ad-Dukhan: 17]

﴿إِنَّهُۥ لَقُرْءَانٌ كَرِيمٌ ٧٧﴾

"This is indeed a holy recitation Ie., the Quran" [TMQ Surah Al-Waqia: 77]

﴿إِنَّكَ أَنتَ ٱلْعَزِيزُ ٱلْكَرِيمُ﴾

"Thou wast the Mighty, the Noble" [TMQ Surah Ad-Dukhan: 49]

﴿رَبُّ ٱلْعَرْشِ ٱلْكَرِيمِ ١١٦﴾

"The Lord of the Throne of grace" [TMQ Surah Al-Muminun: 116]

and

﴿بِرَبِّكَ ٱلْكَرِيمِ ٦﴾

"Thy Lord, the Bountiful" [TMQ Surah Al-Infitar: 6]

Generosity, benevolence. nobility, magnanimity, etc., of God being the perennial themes of the Qur'an, which have been elucidated at countless places in it in different ways, this epithet of the Almighty gives birth to the emotions of loving regard for the Lord and urges man to be himself kind and benevolent to others.

44. The Watcher (Ar-Raqib-o) الرقيب

A. Should always be careful of one's own baser self and the promptings of the Satan.

B. A title of the Divine Being referred to in verses 4:1 and 55:33-

﴿إِنَّ ٱللَّهَ كَانَ عَلَيْكُمْ رَقِيبًا ۝١﴾

"Verily Allah is even a watcher over you. [TMQ Surah An-Nisaa: 1]

Being the Creator and Preserver of all, He is naturally watchful of everything. Nobody should entertain any misconception about His not being aware or overlooking what one does openly or secretly.

45. The Responsive, Answering (Al-Mujib-o) المجيب

A. Should willingly obey Divine commandments.

B. This epithet occurs in verse 11: 61 which runs:

﴿فَٱسْتَغْفِرُوهُ ثُمَّ تُوبُوٓا۟ إِلَيْهِ ۚ إِنَّ رَبِّى قَرِيبٌ مُّجِيبٌ ۝٦١﴾

"Therefore, ask forgiveness of Him, then turn to Him in repentance; verily my Lord is Nigh, Responsive." [TMQ Surah Hud: 61]

This title, like certain other Attributive Names of God, emphasises His mercy, which is ever willing to forgive the sins of His creatures, provided they sincerely repent and make a firm resolve not to commit them again. One should, therefore, respond to divine command and be willing to obey Him.

46. The Bountiful, All-Pervading. (Al-Was'i-o) الواسع

A. One should never be stingy.

B. The title *Wās'i-un* has been used for God in the Qur'an in different contexts, such as,

﴿فَأَيْنَمَا تُوَلُّوا۟ فَثَمَّ وَجْهُ ٱللَّهِ ۚ إِنَّ ٱللَّهَ وَٰسِعٌ عَلِيمٌ ١١٥﴾

"Whither you turn, you would find God All-Pervading."

[TMQ Surah Al-Baqara: 115]

﴿وَٱللَّهُ وَٰسِعٌ عَلِيمٌ ٢٤٧﴾

"God is bountiful (in elevating and exalting any person)."

[TMQ Surah Al-Baqara: 247]

﴿وَٱللَّهُ وَٰسِعٌ عَلِيمٌ ٢٦١﴾

"God is Bountiful in rewarding" [TMQ Surah Al-Baqara: 261]

and

﴿وَٰسِعُ ٱلْمَغْفِرَةِ ۚ﴾

"Of vast forgiveness" [TMQ Surah An-Najm: 32]

Indefinable within the categories of human thought as God is, this epithet suggests that His every Attribute is so vast or capacious that its scope or extent cannot possibly be conceived. We can have some idea of it from verse 31: 27 which says:

﴿وَلَوْ أَنَّمَا فِي ٱلْأَرْضِ مِن شَجَرَةٍ أَقْلَٰمٌ وَٱلْبَحْرُ يَمُدُّهُۥ مِنۢ بَعْدِهِۦ سَبْعَةُ أَبْحُرٍ مَّا نَفِدَتْ كَلِمَٰتُ ٱللَّهِ ۗ إِنَّ ٱللَّهَ عَزِيزٌ حَكِيمٌ ﴿٢٧﴾﴾

"And if whatever trees are on the earth were pens, and sea were ink, with seven more to help it, the words of Allah (i.e., words denoting His excellence, His attributes, and His perfections) could not be exhausted; verily, Allah is Mighty, Wise." [TMQ Surah Luqman: 27]

47. The Wise (Al-Hakim-o) الحكيم

A. One should endeavour to increase his knowledge, experience, and prudence.

B. This Attributive name of God frequently occurs in the Qur'an, e.g.,

﴿إِنَّكَ أَنتَ ٱلْعَزِيزُ ٱلْحَكِيمُ ﴿١٢٩﴾﴾

"Surely, Thou alone art Mighty, Wise" [TMQ Surah Al-Baqara: 129]

God is the Possessor of infinite wisdom who has endowed every man with as much knowledge and prudence as fitted him and accorded his capacity. It also follows that His injunctions to man are full of wisdom for him and the human society.

48. The Loving. The Affectionate (Al-Wadad-o) الودود

A. Should love the righteous.

B. An epithet of God, e.g.,

﴿وَهُوَ ٱلۡغَفُورُ ٱلۡوَدُودُ ١٤﴾

"And He is the Forgiving, Loving." [TMQ Surah Al-Buruj: 14]

A great number of divine attributes are nothing but a manifestation of His love and affection for His creation, particularly man. The affectionate and tender regard God has for man is best illustrated by a hadith related by Abū Huraira from the holy Prophet, which is also a meaningful allegory on God's concern for human welfare.

"Allah will ask someone on the Day of Judgement,' relates Abu Huraira, 'O son of Adam, I fell ill, but you did not come to see Me? Man will reply, 'Allah! Thou wert the Lord of the worlds; How could have I attended Thee?' God will then say, 'Did you not know one of My servants had fallen ill, but you did not go to attend him? Did you not know that if you had attended him, you would have found Me by his side?'

'O son of Adam, I asked for food from you, but you did not give it to Me, God will ask another individual who will answer, 'Allah! Thou wert the Sustainer of the worlds! How could have I fed Thee?" God will then say, 'One of My servants asked you for food, but you refused it to him. Had you fed him, you would have found Me near him!'

'O son of Adam, Fasked for water from you, but you refused it to Me, God will similarly ask again. Man will say in reply, 'Thou wert the Lord of the worlds. How could have I quenched Thy thirst?' God will answer, 'One of My servants demanded water from you but you refused. Had you given him water you would have found Me near him!"

Can there be any better concept of God's tender regard for man.

49. The Glorious, The Illustrious (Al-Majid-o) المجيد

A. One should achieve celebrity through virtuous conduct.

B. Allah is

﴿ذُو ٱلْعَرْشِ ٱلْمَجِيدُ ۝١٥ فَعَّالٌ لِّمَا يُرِيدُ ۝١٦﴾

"Lord of the Throne, the Glorious; Performer of what He wills"

[TMQ Surah Al-Buruj: 15-16]

This attributive name of God portrays His absolute will, dominance and power. 'His is the absolutely sovereign will, unfettered by any conditions or restrictions. Nothing can come between His will and execution. Unlike the head of many a pantheon, who is surrounded by fellow deities and whose will frequently clash with them and who must at times bow to the over-ruling Fate, the God of Islam is all-in-all, Sovereign in absolute sense of the word.' (AM)

50. Sender of the Messengers, Revivifier (Al-Ba'is-o) الباعث

A. Purify one's heart with God's remembrance.

B. The title does not occur in the Qur'an but the revelation from Him reminds man, at several places, that He has, in His mercy, sent messengers to all the nations and communities (10:47, 7:35, 15:10) to deliver His messages (16:36). There are references to the Apostles of God whose names have been mentioned in the Qur'an at numerous places and there have been messengers whose names do not find a place in it (10:74). These messengers were sent by God since He did not want to punish any people before warning them about the consequences of their evil behaviour (6: 130-31).

If one should ponder over the working of natural phenomena, it would be clear to him that the whole system is devised to sustain life on earth. The sun is there to give light and heat and methodically draw out water from the ocean. The winds are there to produce alternately coolness and warmth. Sometimes they weft particles of water up into the skies, and sometimes they reduce these into water again. The earth is there to serve as a perennial storehouse of the means of growth and sustenance, and to offer from within its bosom life to every grain, and growth to every plant. Life's workshop is incessantly engaged in this process. Apart from these material things, there are forces of nature, some of which we have discovered through scientific methods, which have made life possible on this planet. These are all manifestations of divine mercy which has made provision for our material requirements. But there are many other imperceptible needs about which our sense perceptions provide us no knowledge, and among these is the guidance we need to lead a virtuous life on this planet. Only the prophets of God are competent to reveal the nature and attributes of God, His commandments and injunctions, relative qualities of faith and action, good and bad consequences of virtues and vices, merits of the heavenly kingdom, and the doom of infernal regions. The Qur'an tells us:

﴿عَٰلِمُ ٱلْغَيْبِ فَلَا يُظْهِرُ عَلَىٰ غَيْبِهِۦٓ أَحَدًا ٢٦ إِلَّا مَنِ ٱرْتَضَىٰ مِن رَّسُولٍ﴾

"(He is) the Knower of the Unseen, and He reveals unto none His secrets, save unto every messenger whom He had chosen"

[TMQ Surah Al-Jinn: 26-27]

They are the divine Warners unto their people for they put mankind on its guard through exhortation and admonition like a guardian, kind and loving. This grace and mercy of God is indicated by the Attributive Title *Al-Ba'is-o.*

51. The Omnipresent, The Witness (As-Shahid-o) الشهيد

A. Should be ever willing to participate in virtuous deeds.

B. The title frequently occurs in the Qur'an, e. g.,

﴿قُلْ يَٰٓأَهْلَ ٱلْكِتَٰبِ لِمَ تَكْفُرُونَ بِـَٔايَٰتِ ٱللَّهِ وَٱللَّهُ شَهِيدٌ عَلَىٰ مَا تَعْمَلُونَ ٩٨﴾

"Say thou, O people of the Book! why do you deny the revelations of Allah, while Allah is a Witness of what you work."

[TMQ Surah Al-Imran: 98]

'He is Ever-Living, Ever-Present. Witness of all human actions, passions, and motives. If not His love, then His fear and the consciousness of His omniscience ought to prompt one to a life of truth, integrity, and honour.' (AM).

52. The Truth (Al-Haqq-o) الحق

A. Should be persevering in all matters of truth.

﴿فَتَعَٰلَى ٱللَّهُ ٱلْمَلِكُ ٱلْحَقُّ﴾.

"High above all is God, The King, The Truth," [TMQ Surah Ta-ha: 114]

says the Qur'an because God is the only Reality while all other things, the wonderful complexities, gradations and nuances that we find in the world blended in one harmonious whole are His creations obeying the Law laid down by Him None of these has any separate entity of its own, nor can any of these exist by itself it would amount to falsehood to put anything in competition or equality with Him. Mystics have accordingly taken the view that nothing really exists except God, for nothing can be like Him or claim to be His rival or partner. Haq also signifies stability or durability. This epithet of God advances the claim of truth to durability. to its right to prevail over what is *bātil* or false, which is thus bound to disappear.

53. The Trustee (Al-Wakil-o) الوكيل

A. Should be helpful to others.

B. The word *Wakil* lit, means one who takes the care of a thing for another, the witness to a bargain and guardian. Hence, when used with the art. *Al*, it signifies the Disposer of all affairs and Protector of His faithful servants and the One who is able to settle accounts with the enemies. The Qur'anic expressions like

﴿وَقَالُوا۟ حَسْبُنَا ٱللَّهُ وَنِعْمَ ٱلْوَكِيلُ ١٧٣﴾

"Suffices us Allah, and an excellent Trustee is He"

[TMQ Surah Al-Imran: 173]

mean that God, being All-good and All-powerful, all our affairs can best be entrusted to His care. He is the best guardian of all interests. The Qur'an teaches that after taking all humanly possible precautions against one's enemies, one should always put his trust in God, who is more aware of the inner workings of events than any human can conceive. Therefore, in consonance with this divine attribute, every man should act as a trustee and helper unto others.

54. The Mighty, The Strong (Al-Qawī-o) القوي

55. The Firm (Al-Matin-o) المتين

A. Should be strong in faith.

B. God has been described at several places as 'The Mighty', 'The Strong', viz.,

﴿إِنَّ رَبَّكَ هُوَ ٱلْقَوِىُّ ٱلْعَزِيزُ ﴿٦٦﴾﴾

"Verily thy Lord! He is the Strong, the Mighty" [TMQ Surah Hud: 66]

and

﴿إِنَّ ٱللَّهَ هُوَ ٱلرَّزَّاقُ ذُو ٱلْقُوَّةِ ٱلْمَتِينُ ﴿٥٨﴾﴾

"Verily Allah! He is the Provider, Owner of Power, the Firm" [TMQ Surah Az-Zariyat: 58]

God is Almighty; He is able to carry out every part of His will and plan and can also infuse strength in whomsoever He desires. Nothing can escape His grasp, nor can the vicissitudes of things elude His power. He is also Firm i. e., solid and strong, requiring no support from anything. His power is steadfast, the same today as it was yesterday, and will remain so forever. To be short, the effects of His might are innumerable and the objects within His power inconceivable.

56. The Patron, The Helper (Al-Wali-o) الولي

A. Should be a patron of faith.

B. A title often used for God in the sense of Patron, Guardian, and Helper, as in these verses:

﴿وَمَا لَكُم مِّن دُونِ ٱللَّهِ مِن وَلِيٍّ وَلَا نَصِيرٍ ١٠٧﴾

"And for you, there is, besides Allah, no guardian or helper."

[TMQ Surah Al-Baqara: 107]

and

﴿ٱللَّهُ وَلِيُّ ٱلَّذِينَ ءَامَنُواْ﴾

"Allah is the Patron of those who believe" [TMQ Surah Al-Baqara: 257]

Calling God as the Patron, Helper, or Guardian implies that there is nothing else which can be compared to Him in these aspects. The concept of 'patron saints,' 'guardian-angels' or 'saviours' is found in many religions, not necessarily those which are polytheistic, but even those which claim monotheism to be their creed. Islam rejects it altogether and holds that elevating any saint or angel or even a prophet as a helper in such matters as increasing one's sustenance, forgiving of sins, curing anyone from illness, granting a child, or granting salvation amounts to *shirk,* i. e., associating others with God.

57. The Praiseworthy (Al-Hamid-o) الحميد

A. One should try to become deserving of admiration by others.

B. An Attributive Name of God occurring at several places in the Qur'an as,

﴿وَٱعۡلَمُوٓاْ أَنَّ ٱللَّهَ غَنِيٌّ حَمِيدٌ ٢٦٧﴾

"And know that Allah is Self-sufficient, Praiseworthy."

[TMQ Surah Al-Baqara: 267]

Active participle of the root *hamd,* which means not only praise but also implies admiration; and it implies the magnifying or honouring of the object thereof" (LL). God is Praiseworthy because He is perfect in His Person and Attributes; He is the Author of everything that deserves our admiration, and thus it is only He, in the last analysis, who deserves all praises.

58. The Counter (Al-Muhsi-o) المحصي

A. One should remember all his actions.

B. "The Counter", e.g.,

﴿إِنَّا نَحۡنُ نُحۡيِ ٱلۡمَوۡتَىٰ وَنَكۡتُبُ مَا قَدَّمُواْ وَءَاثَٰرَهُمۡۚ وَكُلَّ شَيۡءٍ أَحۡصَيۡنَٰهُ فِيٓ إِمَامٖ مُّبِينٖ ١٢﴾

"Verily We! We shall raise the dead, and We write down what they have forwarded and what they have left behind. And everything We have counted up in a Luminous Record," [TMQ Surah Ya-Sin: 12]

The reason, justice, and morality demand that there should be another life in which a complete account should be taken of what man had done from his maturity until his death and of what his actions have left behind, good or bad, which have influenced generation after generation for a long time after his death. If there was no accountability and no reward for good deeds and punishment for bad deeds, it would mean that this world was without justice and the whole life of man was meaningless, purposeless, and fruitless. Then, in this earthly life, there can be no possibility of complete accountability, justice, or reward and punishment. No intelligent and reasonable man could ever think that this whole planetary system and the life on this earth with man as its perfect specimen were created for nothing, and that everything would end in nothing. Thus, a logical conclusion that follows is that the Creator of man must keep an account of man's actions and require the good and the bad with justice in the afterlife.

﴿فَمَن يَعۡمَلۡ مِثۡقَالَ ذَرَّةٍ خَيۡرٗا يَرَهُۥ ۝٧﴾

"Then whosoever has done good an atom's weight will see it." [TMQ Surah Al-Zalzalah: 7]

This will be made possible by keeping a complete record of everybody's deeds as stated in verses 50: 18 and 82:11.

59. The Originator (Al-Mubdi-o) المبدئ

60. The Restorer. (Al-Mu'id-o) المعيد

A. One should be the first in beginning a good deed and should do it repeatedly.

B. These titles have not been mentioned in the Qur'an, but the idea has been expressed at several places, e.g.,

﴿أَوَ لَمۡ يَرَوۡاْ كَيۡفَ يُبۡدِئُ ٱللَّهُ ٱلۡخَلۡقَ ثُمَّ يُعِيدُهُۥٓۚ إِنَّ ذَٰلِكَ عَلَى ٱللَّهِ يَسِيرٞ ١٩﴾

"Do they not see how Allah originates creation? And then He shall restore it; surely that is easy for Allah" [TMQ Surah Al-Ankabut: 19]

Another verse says:

﴿إِنَّهُۥ هُوَ يُبۡدِئُ وَيُعِيدُ ١٣﴾

"Verily He (it is) Who begins (the creation) and repeats."

[TMQ Surah Al-Buruj: 13]

The originating of creation is the creation of primaeval matter. The repetition of the process of creation goes on constantly, for at every moment new processes are being called into being by the creative power of God, and according to His Laws, And the final creation as far as man is concerned, will be in the *Ma'ad*, when the whole world as man sees it will be entirely newly created on a different plane. As far as God is concerned, there is nothing final- no first and last, for He is infinite.' (AYA). In their wider connotations, origination and recreation signify two events which are constantly taking place. At every moment, there is origination as well as recreation of what has died and decayed in the physical world. The whole universe would appear, on a little more reflection, in a state of continuous renovation, and constant decay.

61. The Quickener (Al-Muhiy-o) المحيي

62. The Killer (Al-Mumit-o) المميت

A. One should quicken his heart by making it perfect and kill his self, i. e., baser desires.

B. God is the sole operator in the matter of life and death- this fact has been repeatedly emphasised in the Qur'an,

﴿رَبِّيَ ٱلَّذِي يُحۡيِۦ وَيُمِيتُ﴾

"My Allah is He who gives life and causes death".

[TMQ Surah Al-Baqara: 258]

﴿وَٱللَّهُ يُحۡيِۦ وَيُمِيتُۗ﴾

"And (it is) Allah (who) makes alive and causes to die."

[TMQ Surah Al-Imran: 156]

﴿فَٱنظُرۡ إِلَىٰٓ ءَاثَٰرِ رَحۡمَتِ ٱللَّهِ كَيۡفَ يُحۡيِ ٱلۡأَرۡضَ بَعۡدَ مَوۡتِهَآۚ إِنَّ ذَٰلِكَ لَمُحۡيِ ٱلۡمَوۡتَىٰۖ وَهُوَ عَلَىٰ كُلِّ شَيۡءٖ قَدِيرٞ ٥٠﴾

"Look then at the effects of Allah's mercy: How He revives the earth after its death, verily He is the Quickener of the dead, and He is Potent over everything." [TMQ Surah Ar-Rum: 50]

If God so wills, He can annihilate the world in a moment, and if He so desires, can recreate it in an instant. Nothing is difficult for Him, whether it be the creation of a fly or that of the seven Heavens. The mysteries of life and death are entirely in His hands: both are His creations, and there is no basis for having separate deities of life and death.

63. The Living (Al Haiy-o) الحي

A. Should strive for the good of eternal life to come.

B. An epithet frequently occurring in the Qur'an, e. g.,

﴿ٱللَّهُ لَآ إِلَٰهَ إِلَّا هُوَ ٱلْحَىُّ ٱلْقَيُّومُ﴾

"Allah! there is no God but He, the Living, the Sustainer.

[TMQ Surah Al-Baqara: 255]

He lives, but His life is self-subsisting and eternal: it does not depend upon other beings and is not limited to time and space. 'Even a fact so patent as the deathlessness of God has needed a clear affirmation in view of the particular sacrifice of heathen gods every spring, as also in view of the 'Christ-God' who suffered death at the hand of his persecutors." (AM). The death of a deity has been a common incident mentioned in the mythologies of many religions.

64. The Sustainer (Al-Qayyūm-o) القيوم

A. Should be firm in the service of God.

B. An Attributive Name frequently occurring in the Qur'an with 'The Living', viz.,

﴿ٱللَّهُ لَآ إِلَٰهَ إِلَّا هُوَ ٱلۡحَيُّ ٱلۡقَيُّومُ ۝٢﴾

"Allah! There is no God but He, the Living, the Sustainer."

[TMQ Surah Al-i'Imran: 2]

One who is self-subsisting and by whom all other things subsist. "By the mere mention of life and self-subsistence as His two essential attributes, the possibility of all co-partnership with Him is negatived outright. Contrast this with the Christian belief that 'the Father is no more God without the Son than the Son is God without Father' (Ency. of Religion and Ethics, VII, p. 536) as also the Hindu belief that certain deities, at any rate, 'are the offspring of others, and that the gods were originally mortal, who have only acquired immortality either by the practice of austerities or by drinking Soma or else by receiving it as gift from Agni and Savita'. (ib. XII, p. 602). Obviously, Islam brushes aside all such absurdities." (AM). This attribute of God perhaps needed to be affirmed in view of the superstitious beliefs that the deities are to be served with articles of food and drink during ritual service to them in order to satisfy and please them. Take for instance the sacrifice which has been a universal element of worship in almost all religions and it has been expressive of a concept of furnishing provisions to God. But the Qur'an contradicts these concepts by saying:

﴿لَن يَنَالَ ٱللَّهَ لُحُومُهَا وَلَا دِمَآؤُهَا وَلَٰكِن يَنَالُهُ ٱلتَّقۡوَىٰ مِنكُمۡۚ﴾

"Their flesh and their blood reach not Allah, but the devotion from you reacheth Him." [TMQ Surah Al-Hajj: 37]

65. The Rich, The Abounding. (Al-Wajid-o) الواجد

A. Should not ask anyone for anything except from God.

B. One of the Excellent Names of God, which does not occur in the Qur'an, but the idea finds a place at several places by laying stress on the fact that everything in the heavens and the earth belongs to God.

﴿وَإِن مِّن شَىْءٍ إِلَّا عِندَنَا خَزَآئِنُهُۥ﴾

"And there is nothing of which there are not with Us treasures.

[TMQ Surah Al-Ḥijr: 21]

says the Qur'an. It simply means that everything that man requires is present with God in an inexhaustible quantity. For every want and every need, it befits man to turn to God instead of demeaning himself by beseeching anyone other than God for his worldly requirements. This epithet is analogous to another Divine title, *Al-Ghani,* occurring in the holy Qur'an.

66. The Glorious, The Noble (Al-Majid-o) الماجد

A. One should attain dignity through self-perfection.

B. The title does not occur in the Qur'an but finds a place in the hadith wherein the Prophet called God by this name also. Its root is the same as that of Majid (no. 49), both the names allude to the same attribute, i. e., Glory and Exaltedness of the Divine Being. It is His will which is Supreme and All-Powerful, and not any abstract cosmic law over which He has relinquished control after creating it. This had been the concept held not by certain ancient philosophical schools, but the view is also subscribed by certain religions and schools of thought today.

67. The One (Al-Wahid-o) الواحد

68. The One (Al-Ahad-o) الأحد

A. Should endeavour to become unique in the service of God.

B. Divine names occurring in the Qur'an:

﴿وَإِلَٰهُكُمْ إِلَٰهٌ وَاحِدٌ﴾

"And your God is the One God (Wahidün)" [TMQ Surah Al-Baqara: 163]

and

﴿قُلْ هُوَ ٱللَّهُ أَحَدٌ ١﴾

"Say thou, He is Allah, the One (Ahad)" [TMQ Surah Al-Ikhlas: 1]

The first alludes to His being unique and perfect in His attributes, while the other to His being One in person and nature. The latter epithet is applied to God alone: 'He who has ever been One and alone; or the indivisible: or He Who has no second to share in His Lordship, nor in His essence, nor in His attributes'. (LL)

'This is monotheism par excellence and not mere monolatry. Verses like the above are meant to emphasise the fact that only One God exists, not that one God is to be worshipped to the exclusion of other gods. This unequivocally repudiates and condemns the Trinity of

Christian godhead, the dualism of the Zoroastrian divinity, and the multiplicity of the gods of polytheistic peoples. (AM).

The Unity of God is the noble theme on which the holy Qur'an lays great stress. There is absolute unity in Divine nature; it admits of no participation or manifoldness in Divine functions. Unity is the keynote to the conception of Divine Being in Islam; it denies all plurality of persons in Godhead and any participation of any being in the affairs of the world. According to *Hitti*, "in this uncompromising monotheism, with its simple, enthusiastic faith in the supreme rule of a transcendent being, lies the chief strength of Islam as a religion" (History of the Arabs, p. 129).

69. The Independent, The Absolute, The Eternal - As-Samad - الصمد

A. Should become so perfect in spirit that everybody may seek guidance from him.

B. Samad is difficult to translate by one word. It may be independent of everyone, and yet be sought of all, i. e., lacking in nothing and wanting none to complement Him; the Absolute; the Eternal. Thus, it negates the idea of gods and goddesses who ate and drank, wrangled and plotted, and depended on the gifts of worshippers, powers *(verdan)* granted by other gods, etc. The epithet applied to God signifies 'A Lord: because one repairs, betakes himself or has recourse, to him, in exigencies, or, when applied to God, because affairs are stayed, or rested, upon Him and none but He accomplishes them......or the Being that continues, or continues forever, or is everlasting; or the Creator of everything, of whom nothing is independent, and whose unity everything indicates.' (LL).

The holy Prophet is reported to have said when asked what *As-Samad* was: 'He is the Lord to whom recourse is had in every need. The statement implies that nothing is independent of Him, and it aims at the correction of the error of those who consider that certain things, such as matter and soul, had existed independently of the Creator. This doctrine is subscribed to by certain polytheistic creeds. It also corrects the error of associating anyone, such as the Son, with the Father, to complete the Godhead.

70. The Able (Al-Qadir-o) القادر

71. The Potent (Al-Muqtadir-o) المقتدر

A. One should exercise control over one's baser desires.

B. Divine epithets occurring in the Qur'an, viz.,

﴿أَوَ لَمْ يَرَوْا أَنَّ ٱللَّهَ ٱلَّذِى خَلَقَ ٱلسَّمَٰوَٰتِ وَٱلْأَرْضَ قَادِرٌ عَلَىٰٓ أَن يَخْلُقَ مِثْلَهُمْ﴾

"Do they not see that Allah who created the heavens and the earth is Able (Qadirün) to create their likes" [TMQ Surah Israel: 99]

﴿وَكَانَ ٱللَّهُ عَلَىٰ كُلِّ شَىْءٍ مُّقْتَدِرًا ﴿٤٥﴾﴾

"And Allah is Potent (Muqtadirün) over everything"

[TMQ Surah Al-Kahf: 45]

Both titles may signify the same possessing power or ability, signifying one who does what he will, according to what wisdom requires and without any let or hindrance from any quarter. Normally, these epithets are employed by the Qur'an to drive home the fact that God has power over everything. He gives life and also death; He causes the rise and downfall, and it is by His command that anything happens in the world. Therefore, one should not forget Him who has bestowed prosperity and can change it into poverty, and vice versa. If one keeps this fact before him, one will never do any wrong to others. He will exercise control over his desires which incite him for their fulfilment at every cost or in any manner.

72. The Advancer (Al-Muqaddim-o) المقدم

73. The Deferrer (Al-Mu'akhkhir-o) المؤخر

A. One should be leading in obedience to God and put off wrongdoing.

B. These epithets do not occur in the Qur'an. They, however, allude to the absolute power of God and man's utter helplessness before him. Let alone doing any good or harm, man, or for that matter any other being, is incapable of hastening or delaying any benefit or loss. The Qur'an says,

﴿إِنَّ رَبَّكَ فَعَّالٌ لِّمَا يُرِيدُ﴾

"Verily thy Lord is the Doer of whatever He intends."

[TMQ Surah Hud: 107]

He can do anything without any let or hindrance on the part of anyone. The God of Islam is the absolute ruler of the world and man. All the natural phenomena and laws are subordinate to His will, and nobody can in any way interfere or intercede with Him.

74. The First	(Al-Awwal-o)	الأول
75. The Last	(Al-Akhir-o)	الآخر
76. The Evident.	(Az-Zahir-o)	الظاهر
77. The Immanent	(Al-Batin-o)	الباطن

A. Should be first in matters relating to religion but last in worldly affairs; conform to the law in one's behaviour and attain the perfection of spirit.

B. The Qur'an refers to all four epithets beautifully in verse 57:3 which reads:

﴿هُوَ ٱلْأَوَّلُ وَٱلْءَاخِرُ وَٱلظَّٰهِرُ وَٱلْبَاطِنُ ۖ وَهُوَ بِكُلِّ شَىْءٍ عَلِيمٌ ۝٣﴾

"He is the First and the Last, and the Evident and the Immanent, and He is Knower of everything. [TMQ Surah Al-Hadid: 3]

The First signifies Eternal, without beginning i. e., prior to every other existing entity. Similarly, the Last suggests that He shall survive all existing entities, is Everlasting and without end. Evident means Manifest in regard to His attributes or self-evident in respect of the fact of His existence, while Immanent implies that He is transcendent in regard to His person or subtle in respect of the nature of His existence. The pair of seemingly opposite qualities, First and Last, Evident and Immanent, Power and Wisdom, Giving of life and death, etc., are referred to here to point to the contrast of our human frailty, in which monasticism may not be the same as humility, spending may not be the same as charity, and so on." (AYA).

In a supplication recorded by Imam Ahmad, Muslim, Tirmidhi, and Baihaqi on the authority of Abu Huraira, the holy Prophet is reported to have said that:

Thou art the First, nothing existed before Thee, Thou art the Last, there shall be nothing after Thee. Thou art the Evident, there is nothing above Thee, Thou art the Immanent, there is nothing hidden from Thee. The Qur'an also speaks of the eternal life of the hereafter, but that should not create any doubt since it also says: 'Everything will perish except His own Face," i.e., the only reality is God. The whole phenomenal world is subject to flux and change and will pass away, but God will endure forever.

78. The Protector, The Ruler (Al-Wali-o) الوالي

A. One should have command over one's self.

B. This epithet has been taken from the Qur'anic verse:

﴿ وَمَا لَهُم مِّن دُونِهِۦ مِن وَالٍ ١١ ﴾

"Nor is for them any Protector besides Him."

[TMQ Surah Ar-Ra'd: 11]

The reference is to the people who do not change themselves and in consequence of their persistent unruliness, draw upon themselves the Divine wrath, and then there is none to hold it back from them. The meaning is obvious: God is the last refuge of man, and there is no intercessor or patron or guardian who can intervene in the will of God.

79. The Exalted, The High (Al-Muta-ali-o) المتعالي

A. Should dominate over the devil within oneself.

B. The title occurs in the Qur'an:

﴿عَٰلِمُ ٱلْغَيْبِ وَٱلشَّهَٰدَةِ ٱلْكَبِيرُ ٱلْمُتَعَالِ ﴿٩﴾﴾

"Knower of the hidden and the manifest! The Great! The Exalted!"

[TMQ Surah Ar-Ra'd: 9]

The epithet means 'one above the description of the attributes of the created being'. God is beyond all definitions- transcending every concept and every form- the attributes employed to describe His majesty do not impose any limitation inherent in human speech. Just as God completely dominates over everything, man ought to exercise control over his predilections and desires. Theories like 'irresistible impulse' advanced for explaining away certain crimes are rejected by Islam.

80. The Benign (Al-Barr-o) البر

A. Should be beneficial to all.

B. The epithet occurs in the Qur'an:

﴿إِنَّهُۥ هُوَ ٱلْبَرُّ ٱلرَّحِيمُ ﴿٢٨﴾﴾

"Verily He! it is He the Benign, the Merciful." [TMQ Surah At-Tur: 28]

The Divine title invites attention to the basic factor in human relationships that mutual generosity in dealing with one another is necessary, for it would be in keeping with this Divine Attribute. Social life cannot be cordial, friendly, and happy if each and every individual insists on his or her own rights. This Attributive Name points to the need of being lenient and generous in dealings with one another. In another verse, the Qur'an exhorts the believers:

﴿وَأَن تَعْفُوٓاْ أَقْرَبُ لِلتَّقْوَىٰۚ وَلَا تَنسَوُاْ ٱلْفَضْلَ بَيْنَكُمْۚ إِنَّ ٱللَّهَ بِمَا تَعْمَلُونَ بَصِيرٌ ٢٣٧﴾

"And if you act generously, it is nearer to piety. Do not forget to show generosity in your dealings with one another, for God sees what you do."

[TMQ Surah Al-Baqara: 237]

81. The Relenting (At-Tawwab-o) التواب

A. Should be ever-willing to forgive others.

B. A title frequently used in the Qur'an viz.,

﴿فَتَلَقَّىٰٓ ءَادَمُ مِن رَّبِّهِۦ كَلِمَٰتٍ فَتَابَ عَلَيْهِۚ إِنَّهُۥ هُوَ ٱلتَّوَّابُ ٱلرَّحِيمُ ٣٧﴾

"Surely it is He Who is Relenting, Merciful."

[TMQ Surah Al-Baqara: 37]

So, it is to God that one must always turn in repentance, as He is ever willing to forgive the sins of the repentant.

The Qur'an says at another place

﴿۞ قُلْ يَٰعِبَادِيَ ٱلَّذِينَ أَسْرَفُوا۟ عَلَىٰٓ أَنفُسِهِمْ لَا تَقْنَطُوا۟ مِن رَّحْمَةِ ٱللَّهِ ۚ إِنَّ ٱللَّهَ يَغْفِرُ ٱلذُّنُوبَ جَمِيعًا ۚ إِنَّهُۥ هُوَ ٱلْغَفُورُ ٱلرَّحِيمُ ﴿٥٣﴾﴾

"Say thou. My bondsmen who have committed extravagance against themselves; despair not of the mercy of Allah: Verily Allah will forgive the sins altogether. Verily, He is the Forgiving. The Merciful."

[TMQ Surah Az-Zumar: 53]

The reason for repeating this attribute of God frequently is to emphasise that 'the God of Islam, unlike the God of so many religions, is neither jealous nor vindictive. This required frequent reiteration not only in view of the doctrines of pagans but also of the teaching of the Bible, 'Beware of him, and obey his voice, provoke him not for he will not pardon your transgressions' (Ex. 23: 21) 'He is Holy God he is a jealous God; he will not forgive your transgressions nor your sins (Jo. 24:19)' (MA).

Forgiveness, being a part of Mercy, such a merit has been attached to it that the believers are implored to forgive and bear the excesses against them. patiently for it is good for them and meritorious in the sight of God. The Qur'an says:

﴿وَإِنْ عَاقَبْتُمْ فَعَاقِبُوا۟ بِمِثْلِ مَا عُوقِبْتُم بِهِۦ ۖ وَلَئِن صَبَرْتُمْ لَهُوَ خَيْرٌ لِّلصَّٰبِرِينَ ﴿١٢٦﴾ وَٱصْبِرْ وَمَا صَبْرُكَ إِلَّا بِٱللَّهِ ۚ وَلَا تَحْزَنْ عَلَيْهِمْ وَلَا تَكُ فِى ضَيْقٍ مِّمَّا يَمْكُرُونَ ﴿١٢٧﴾﴾

"If you retaliate, then retaliate to the same extent that ye were injured; but if ye can endure patiently, best will it be for those who patiently endure. "Endure thou with patience. The endurance is only by (the help of) Allah."

[TMQ Surah An-Nahl: 126-127]

82. The Avenger (Al-Muntaqim-o) المنتقم

A. There should be no let up while avenging for the sake of God.

B.

﴿وَمَنْ أَظْلَمُ مِمَّن ذُكِّرَ بِـَٔايَٰتِ رَبِّهِۦ ثُمَّ أَعْرَضَ عَنْهَآ ۚ إِنَّا مِنَ ٱلْمُجْرِمِينَ مُنتَقِمُونَ ﴿٢٢﴾﴾

"And who is a great wrong-doer than he who is reminded of His signs, and he turns aside therefrom? Verily We are going to be Avenger unto the culprits." [TMQ Surah As-Sajda: 22]

The title in this verse, as well as in verses 43: 41 and 44: 16 alludes to the punishment of the wrongdoers on the Day of Judgement. The whole philosophy of life unfolded by the Qur'an is that this world has not been created by God for play or sport with no wisdom behind it, or with no purpose or object. Man has not been left on his own to do whatever he likes without having to answer for his actions. For the good and the bad cannot be the same in the sight of God, the good must be rewarded, and those who reject the commandments of God and spread evil and corruption in this world must be punished in the Hereafter. God has appointed a Day for that purpose when each soul will be retributed justly for his actions. And who can be a better 'Avenger' of misdeeds than God, who is fully aware of our actions and their results?

83. The Pardoning (Al-Afuw-o) العفو

A. Should pardon others as much as possible.

B.

﴿إِنَّ ٱللَّهَ كَانَ عَفُوًّا غَفُورًا ﴿٤٣﴾﴾

"Verily Allah is ever Pardoning, Forgiving" [TMQ Surah An-Nisaa: 43]

says the Qur'an to emphasise Divine Mercy. *'Afü* means 'to erase' or to 'blot out' besides 'to pardon' and 'to pass over. These epithets employed in the Qur'an really allude to the fact that the gates of Divine Mercy are always open for sinners and invite them to seek pardon from God for their temporary deviations from the right path. Describing the clemency of God Who is ever-willing to forgive the sinners, the Qur'an employs an alluringly charming diction inviting those who have deviated from the path of virtue to return broken in spirit with a sense of guilt to God, and they would find that the sympathy, magnanimity, and mercy of God are at hand to exonerate their sins. Divine forgiveness driven home through a number of Attributive Names is meant to do away with the misery and suffering the human race had to endure because of the doctrines of the inherent sinfulness of man upheld by several religions. The monastic orders of the Medieval Ages had developed these with an appealing vividness. The humanity scared by these ghastly visions and glimpses of eternal suffering felt relieved by Islam's emphasis on God's all-embracing mercy and the efficacy of repentance. The Prophet was never tired of telling the people how God was Very-Forgiving; that His love for man was more tender than that of the mother bird for her young. He also taught man to forget and forgive others as a means of attaining propinquity to God.

84. The Tender (Ar-Ra'uf-o) الرؤوف

A. Should have tender regard for the God-fearing.

B. Yet another epithet of the Supreme Being, manifesting another aspect of His mercy. This title has been frequently used in the Qur'an as, e.g.,

﴿إِنَّ ٱللَّهَ بِٱلنَّاسِ لَرَءُوفٌ رَّحِيمٌ ١٤٣﴾

"Surely Allah is to mankind Tender, Merciful."

[TMQ Surah Al-Baqara: 143]

i.e., He has solicitude, tender regard, and compassionate care for them. Divine mercy is such a recurring theme of the Qur'an that it would be no exaggeration to identify the Divine concept presented by it as the 'God of Mercy'. Divine grace is not limited to any particular people, race, or nation. It is common to the entire human race. The object of drawing attention to the different aspects of divine mercy and compassion, which really permeates a large number of other attributes and imparts them a qualifying touch, is to ask the people to develop this quality in themselves. Here are a few such examples.

﴿۞ لَّيْسَ ٱلْبِرَّ أَن تُوَلُّوا۟ وُجُوهَكُمْ قِبَلَ ٱلْمَشْرِقِ وَٱلْمَغْرِبِ وَلَـٰكِنَّ ٱلْبِرَّ مَنْ ءَامَنَ بِٱللَّهِ وَٱلْيَوْمِ ٱلْـَٔاخِرِ وَٱلْمَلَـٰٓئِكَةِ وَٱلْكِتَـٰبِ وَٱلنَّبِيِّـۧنَ وَءَاتَى ٱلْمَالَ عَلَىٰ حُبِّهِۦ ذَوِى ٱلْقُرْبَىٰ وَٱلْيَتَـٰمَىٰ وَٱلْمَسَـٰكِينَ وَٱبْنَ ٱلسَّبِيلِ وَٱلسَّآئِلِينَ وَفِى ٱلرِّقَابِ وَأَقَامَ ٱلصَّلَوٰةَ وَءَاتَى ٱلزَّكَوٰةَ وَٱلْمُوفُونَ بِعَهْدِهِمْ إِذَا عَـٰهَدُوا۟ ۖ وَٱلصَّـٰبِرِينَ فِى ٱلْبَأْسَآءِ وَٱلضَّرَّآءِ وَحِينَ ٱلْبَأْسِ ۗ أُو۟لَـٰٓئِكَ ٱلَّذِينَ صَدَقُوا۟ ۖ وَأُو۟لَـٰٓئِكَ هُمُ ٱلْمُتَّقُونَ ١٧٧﴾

"Virtue is not (in this) that you turn your faces to the east and the west, but virtue is of (him) who believes in Allah and the Last Day and the angels and the Book, and the prophets, and gives (of his) substance, for love of Him, to the kindred orphans and the needy and the wayfarer and the beggers and for (redeeming) necks". [TMQ Surah Al-Baqara: 177]

﴿وَيُطْعِمُونَ ٱلطَّعَامَ عَلَىٰ حُبِّهِۦ مِسْكِينًا وَيَتِيمًا وَأَسِيرًا ﴿٨﴾ إِنَّمَا نُطْعِمُكُمْ لِوَجْهِ ٱللَّهِ لَا نُرِيدُ مِنكُمْ جَزَآءً وَلَا شُكُورًا ﴿٩﴾﴾

"And they feed, for love of Him, with food the destitute, the orphan and the captives-(saying) We feed you only for the sake of Allah; we desire not from you (any) recompense or thanks" [TMQ Surah Ad-Dahr: 8-9]

85. Sovereign of the Dominion, Owner of Majesty and Beneficence.

مالك الملك ذو الجلال والاكرام *(Malik-ul-Mulk-i-Zul-jalal-i-wal-Ikrami)*

A. One should become a master of His own self and show respect to the God-fearing.

B. An epithet of God occurring in the Qur'an (3: 26,55: 27, 78) means that the Divine Being is full of Majesty, Bounty, and Honour. 'Two ideas are prominent in the word *Ikram*, (1) the idea of generosity, as proceeding from the person whose attribute it is, and (2) the idea of honour, as given by others to the person whose attribute it is' (AYA). God of Islam, the 'Owner of Majesty and Beneficence' is never distant and remote from man in spite of His Glory, Power, and Transcendence. 'He is the constant companion of His servants, their unfailing support and an infallible prop to those in need and distress- unlike so many gods of polytheism elevated far above man, living in Olympian heights and having little or no vital connection with them.' (MA) God is always willing to answer the call of man:

﴿وَإِذَا سَأَلَكَ عِبَادِى عَنِّى فَإِنِّى قَرِيبٌ أُجِيبُ دَعْوَةَ ٱلدَّاعِ إِذَا دَعَانِ فَلْيَسْتَجِيبُوا۟ لِى وَلْيُؤْمِنُوا۟ بِى لَعَلَّهُمْ يَرْشُدُونَ ﴿١٨٦﴾﴾

"And when My bondmen ask thee (O Prophet) regarding Me, then surely I am nigh. I listen to the prayer of every suppliant when he calls on Me; so let them listen to My call and believe in Me; (so) that they may walk in the right path." [TMQ Surah Al-Baqara: 186]

His all-pervading character, which is independent of all conditions of time and space, and intimacy with His creatures has been alluded to in certain other verses which read:

﴿وَنَحْنُ أَقْرَبُ إِلَيْهِ مِنْ حَبْلِ ٱلْوَرِيدِ ﴿١٦﴾﴾

"We are nearer to him than his jugular vein" [TMQ Surah Qaf: 16]

and

﴿وَهُوَ مَعَكُمْ أَيْنَ مَا كُنتُمْ﴾

"He is with you wherever you may be." [TMQ Al-Hadid: 4]

86. The Equitable. (Al-Muqsit-o) المقسط

A. One should be just to others.

B. A title of God not occurring in the Qur'an but mentioned in the hadith. Two other names alluding to the justice of God are *Al-Hakam-o* and *Al-'Adl o* (No. 29 and 30). Justice and benevolence are the two qualities which have been commended repeatedly by the Qur'an. In *Sürah Al-Nahl,* we read:

﴿۞إِنَّ ٱللَّهَ يَأۡمُرُ بِٱلۡعَدۡلِ وَٱلۡإِحۡسَٰنِ وَإِيتَآيِٕ ذِى ٱلۡقُرۡبَىٰ﴾

"God commanded justice, the doing of good and liberality to kith and kin."

[TMQ Surah An-Nahl: 90]

It commands people to do justice even to their enemies.

﴿يَٰٓأَيُّهَا ٱلَّذِينَ ءَامَنُواْ كُونُواْ قَوَّٰمِينَ لِلَّهِ شُهَدَآءَ بِٱلۡقِسۡطِۖ وَلَا يَجۡرِمَنَّكُمۡ شَنَـَٔانُ قَوۡمٍ عَلَىٰٓ أَلَّا تَعۡدِلُواْۚ ٱعۡدِلُواْ هُوَ أَقۡرَبُ لِلتَّقۡوَىٰۖ﴾

"O you who believe! Be steadfast witnesses for God in equity, and let not hatred of any people seduce you that you deal not justly. Deal justly, that is nearer to piety." [TMQ Surah Al-Maidah: 8]

Again, in Sürah al-An'am we read,

﴿وَإِذَا قُلۡتُمۡ فَٱعۡدِلُواْ وَلَوۡ كَانَ ذَا قُرۡبَىٰۖ﴾

"Whenever you speak, speak justly, even if a near relative is concerned."

[TMQ Surah Al-An'am: 152]

Many more verses of the Qur'an can be cited in which the believers have been commanded to administer justice with complete impartiality since God is Himself the Best of all Judges.

﴿إِنَّ ٱللَّهَ لَا يَظۡلِمُ مِثۡقَالَ ذَرَّةٖۖ﴾

"Surely Allah does not wrong anyone a grain's weight"

[TMQ Surah An-Nisaa: 40]

and

﴿فَلَا تُظْلَمُ نَفْسٌ شَيْـًٔا ۖ وَإِن كَانَ مِثْقَالَ حَبَّةٍ مِّنْ خَرْدَلٍ﴾

"No one will be wronged at all if it be the weight of a grain of mustard seed."
[TMQ Surah Al-Anbiyaa: 47]

87. The Assembler (Al-Jam'i-o) الجامع

A. One should combine knowledge with virtuous deeds.

B. A Divine name occurring in the Qur'an,

﴿رَبَّنَآ إِنَّكَ جَامِعُ ٱلنَّاسِ لِيَوْمٍ لَّا رَيْبَ فِيهِ ۚ﴾

"Our Lord: surely Thou art the Assembler of mankind on a Day of which there is no doubt," [TMQ Surah Al-Imran: 9]

and

﴿إِنَّ ٱللَّهَ جَامِعُ ٱلْمُنَٰفِقِينَ وَٱلْكَٰفِرِينَ فِى جَهَنَّمَ جَمِيعًا ﴿١٤٠﴾﴾

"Verily Allah is about to gather hypocrites and infidels in Hell together.
[TMQ Surah An-Nisaa: 140]

The 'Assembler' in these verses means that God will resurrect all who had once lived and had died in order to require them for their actions. In several verses, the Qur'än has referred to the doubts of those who think that resurrection on the Day of Judgement is impossible and given convincing reasons that it will not at all be difficult for Him to bring them to life again e. g., in verses 17: 49-52, 19:66-67, 22: 5 etc.

88. The Self-Sufficing (Al-Ghani-o) الغني

89. The Enricher, (Al-Mughni-o) المغني

A. One should be independent of the other, but help others in their needs.

B. The epithet Al-Ghani occurs in the Qur'an at several places, viz.,

﴿وَٱعۡلَمُوٓاْ أَنَّ ٱللَّهَ غَنِيٌّ حَمِيدٌ ٢٦٧﴾

"And know that Allah is Self-sufficing, Praiseworthy."

[TMQ Surah Al-Baqara: 267]

Both the Divine names are derived from the same root meaning to be rich, independent, or in the comfort of life. Surely God is independent of all wants, and He has no need of any presents or oblations. On the other hand. He can enrich anyone out of His benevolence. Both these names express the independence of the Supreme Being from the necessities and requirements of mankind and His ability to grant whatever He wants to anyone. Another name of the Almighty carrying an analogous sense is As-Samad (no. 69). All these attributes point to the fact that God is Absolute and Independent. To Him are to be addressed all supplications, and only He is capable of answering the prayers of his servants.

90. The Withholder (Al-Man'i-o) المانع

A. One should not spend lavishly on occasions not enjoined by the *Shari'ah.*

B. An epithet which does not occur in the Qur'an but is to be found in the hadith. God withholds or does not grant our prayer on certain occasions as He, in His infinite wisdom, knows what is good or bad for us.

﴿وَيَدْعُ ٱلْإِنسَٰنُ بِٱلشَّرِّ دُعَآءَهُۥ بِٱلْخَيْرِ ۖ وَكَانَ ٱلْإِنسَٰنُ عَجُولًا ﴿١١﴾﴾

"And man prays for evil as he should pray for good, and man is ever hasty" [TMQ Surah Israel: 11]

says the Qur'an. Were God to grant all the prayers of man, he would be doomed because of his ignorance and hasty nature. It is a common experience that we sometimes consider something good for us, but it turns out to be harmful. Thus, the decision of God to withhold or deny something coveted by us is also out of His mercy, although we do not perceive it at the moment.

91. The Distresser (Az-Zarr-o) الضار

A. One should inflict harm on the enemies of God.

B. There is no harm or good which befalls man save with the will and command of God. The title does not occur in the Qur'an, but the idea is to be found in several verses.

﴿وَإِن يَمْسَسْكَ ٱللَّهُ بِضُرٍّ فَلَا كَاشِفَ لَهُۥٓ إِلَّا هُوَ ۖ وَإِن يُرِدْكَ بِخَيْرٍ فَلَا رَآدَّ لِفَضْلِهِۦ ۚ
يُصِيبُ بِهِۦ مَن يَشَآءُ مِنْ عِبَادِهِۦ ۚ وَهُوَ ٱلْغَفُورُ ٱلرَّحِيمُ ﴿١٠٧﴾﴾

"And if Allah touches thee with hurt, there is no remover thereof but He, and if He intends any good, there is no averter of His grace. He lets. it befalls on

whomsoever of His bondmen He will: and He is the Forgiving, Merciful."
[TMQ Surah Yunus: 107]

And again,

﴿إِنَّمَا ٱلنَّجْوَىٰ مِنَ ٱلشَّيْطَٰنِ لِيَحْزُنَ ٱلَّذِينَ ءَامَنُوا۟ وَلَيْسَ بِضَآرِّهِمْ شَيْـًٔا إِلَّا بِإِذْنِ ٱللَّهِ ۚ وَعَلَى ٱللَّهِ فَلْيَتَوَكَّلِ ٱلْمُؤْمِنُونَ ۝١٠﴾

"Whispering is only from Satan that he may grieve the believers; and he cannot harm them at all save with the leave of Allah. So, in Allah let the faithful trust" [TMQ Surah Al-Mujadila: 10]

'Evil can harm no one who is good, except in so far as (1) there is some question of trial in God's Universal Plan, or (2) what appears to be harm may be really good. Nothing happens without God's will and permission. And we must always trust Him, and not our cleverness or any adventitious circumstances that draw us the least bit from the path of rectitude.' (AYA).

92. The Benefactor (An-Nafi-o) النافع

A. Should cause benefit to those who tread the righteous path.

B. The epithet does not occur in the Qur'an, but the idea is found in a number of verses. Here are a few examples.

﴿قُلْ أَنَدْعُوا۟ مِن دُونِ ٱللَّهِ مَا لَا يَنفَعُنَا وَلَا يَضُرُّنَا﴾

"Say thou: shall we call upon besides Allah, what can neither profit us nor hurt us." [TMQ Surah Al-Anʿām: 71]

and

﴿قُلْ أَتَعْبُدُونَ مِن دُونِ ٱللَّهِ مَا لَا يَمْلِكُ لَكُمْ ضَرًّا وَلَا نَفْعًا﴾

"He said: do not worship them besides Allah, what can neither profit you nor hurt you." [TMQ Surah Al-Mā'idah: 76]

It is manifestly clear that:

﴿إِنَّهُۥ هُوَ ٱلْبَرُّ ٱلرَّحِيمُ ۝٢٨﴾

"Truly it is He, the Beneficent, the Merciful" [TMQ Surah At-Tur: 28]

﴿مَن يَرْزُقُكُم مِّنَ ٱلسَّمَآءِ وَٱلْأَرْضِ﴾

"who gives us sustenance" [TMQ Surah Yunus: 31]

﴿ذُو ٱلْفَضْلِ ٱلْعَظِيمِ﴾

"is the Lord of Bounties" [TMQ Surah Al-Jumu'a: 4]

﴿۞ قُلْ مَن يَرْزُقُكُم مِّنَ ٱلسَّمَٰوَٰتِ وَٱلْأَرْضِ﴾

"and who provides gifts from the heavens and earth."

[TMQ Surah al-Saba: 24]

﴿وَإِن تَعُدُّوا۟ نِعْمَتَ ٱللَّهِ لَا تُحْصُوهَآ﴾

"As a matter of fact, nobody can count the favours of God"

[TMQ Surah Ibrahim: 34]

as his bounties and favours to man are illimitable and innumerable.

93. The Light (An-Nür-o) النور

One should illuminate oneself with the light of faith and divine knowledge.

B. A title of Almighty meaning the light, faith, divine wisdom, and revelation from God (viz. 2:17,257,5:44 and 4:175).

This Divine Name has been taken from the verse 35 of the 24th Chapter *Surat-un-Nür,* which is incomparable in grandeur and diction.

"God is Light.
Of the heavens and the earth.
The parable of His Light
Is as if there were a Niche
And within it a Lamp:
The Lamp enclosed in Glass,
The glass as it were
A brilliant star:
Lit from a blessed Tree,
An Olive, neither of the East,
Nor of the West,
Whose oil is well-nigh
Luminous,
Though fire scarce touched it:
Light upon Light!
God doth guide
Whom He will
To His Light:

God doth set forth Parables
For men, and God
Doth know all things".

'Glorious, illimitable Light, cannot be described or measured. And there are grades and grades of it, passing transcendently into regions of spiritual height, which man's imagination can scarcely conceive of. The topmost pinnacle is the true prototypal Light, the real Light, of which all others were reflections, the Light of God. Hence, the saying of the holy Prophet about God's Seventy thousand veils of Light. (AYA).

Nur or light, is that which manifests hidden things, and Allah is called here the Light of the heavens and the earth because He has manifested them and brought them into existence. The Qur'an always speaks of *An-Nür* only in its singular form, which indicates that the source of divine Light or guidance is only one. As Dr. Iqbal says the metaphor of Light as applied to God must, in view of modern knowledge, be taken to suggest the Absoluteness of God.

94. The Guide (Al-Hadi-o) الهادي

A. Should continue to guide the evil-doers on the right path.

B. The title does not occur in the Qur'an, but the verb occurs at several places to suggest that it is God alone who guides man.

﴿ يَهْدِى مَن يَشَآءُ إِلَىٰ صِرَٰطٍ مُّسْتَقِيمٍ ﴿١٤٢﴾ ﴾

"He guides whom He will to the straight path,"

[TMQ Surah Al-Baqara: 142]

and

﴿وَٱللَّهُ لَا يَهْدِى ٱلْقَوْمَ ٱلظَّٰلِمِينَ ٢٥٨﴾

"Allah guides not the wrongdoers," [TMQ Surah Al-Baqara: 258]

are some of the examples. It is to be noted that the verses speaking of divine guidance make it clear that divine guidance is available only to those who have a disposition for it and obey the divine command. Disobedience and transgression, when formed as a habit by the sinners and rejectors of truth, deaden the desire to know what is truth. They are then not allowed to take advantage of divine guidance.

95. The Originator (Al-Bad'i-o) البديع

A. Should endeavour to find out new ways to follow the Straight Path.

B. God is

﴿بَدِيعُ ٱلسَّمَٰوَٰتِ وَٱلْأَرْضِ ۖ وَإِذَا قَضَىٰٓ أَمْرًا فَإِنَّمَا يَقُولُ لَهُۥ كُن فَيَكُونُ ١١٧﴾

"The Originator of the heavens and the earth; and whenever He desires an affair, He merely says it: 'be', and it becomes."[TMQ Surah Al-Baqara: 117]

'Bad'i is the Originator of the creation, according to His own will, not after the similitude of anything pre-existing." (LL). He is thus the absolute Author, not a mere manufacturer or designer as conceived by several pagan peoples-Independent of any or every material or pattern. Even the Jews, under the influence of Alexandrian philosophy and swayed by Platonic and Neoplatonic ideas, had come

to regard the act of creation as carried into effect through intermediate agencies, sub-deities, as it were, with independent existence and will of their own.'(AM) The 'affair' referred to in the above verse includes abstract as well as material things. The Islamic concept of God thus sets at naught the ideas that the creation of anything by God is dependent on the previous existence of matter and soul and the adaptability of their attributes.

96. The Everlasting (Al-Baqi-o) الباقي

A. Should do works that will be of benefit after one dies.

B. The title does not occur in the Qur'an, but the root from which it is derived means remaineth, lasteth permanently, or more lasting. The Qur'an says:

﴿وَٱللَّهُ خَيْرٌ وَأَبْقَىٰٓ ٧٣﴾

"And Allah is Best and Most Abiding." [TMQ Surah Ta-ha: 73]

God being ever-lasting, He shall remain when everything conceivable has perished.

97. The Heir (Al-Waris-o) الوارث

A. Should endeavour to inherit the knowledge brought by the prophets of God.

B. Yet another title of the Almighty, though not occurring in the Qur'an, to indicate that He is the Last, The Everlasting. It may also mean that everything we possess or find in this world will ultimately revert back to God. Actually, speaking whatever we have and claim to be ours is just held in trust for a limited period since

﴿وَلِلَّهِ مِيرَٰثُ ٱلسَّمَٰوَٰتِ وَٱلْأَرْضِ﴾

"to God belongs the heritage of the heavens and the earth."

[TMQ Surah Al-Imran: 180]

98. The Right-Minded (Ar-Rashid-o) الرشيد

A. Should direct the people to the right course of action.

B. The epithet does not occur in the Qur'an for God. It suggests that a man without any knowledge of the future and unable to foresee the result of his actions should depend on God, who can alone help him to take the right course. The title has been used in the hadith.

99. The Patient (As-Sabūr-o) الصبور

A. One should be patient in difficulties.

B. Sabara, the root from which this title has been derived, means to endure, to be patient. Although the title does not occur in the Qur'an, the idea occurs frequently. The Qur'an describes God as the Most Forbearing (c.f., 2: 225, 235, 263; 3: 155, etc.) who never punishes the infidels and sinners immediately and even continues to provide them with His favours, leaving the punishment for the Hereafter. The Qur'an repeatedly impresses upon man, as this Divine title also suggests, to be patient in difficulties and show perseverance and constancy in good works and righteousness.

www.ingramcontent.com/pod-product-compliance
Ingram Content Group UK Ltd.
Pitfield, Milton Keynes, MK11 3LW, UK
UKHW021410190726
13845UKWH00028B/989

9 789394 770805